THE SEVEN HEBREW EPISTLES:

DISPENSATIONALLY CONSIDERED

James	1 Peter	2 Peter
1 John	2 John	3 John
	Jude	

A GRACE EXPOSITIONAL COMMENTARY

SECOND EDITION

DR. DAVID ALAN GREENE

GraceWord Publishing, LLC
www.gracewordpublishing.com
U.S.A.

GRACEWORD PUBLISHING

Contents

To The Twelve Tribes
Scattered Abroad
And All Who Follow
The Gospel Of The Kingdom

And then shall many be offended,
and shall betray one another,
and shall hate one another.
And many false prophets shall rise,
and shall deceive many.
And because iniquity shall abound,
the love of many shall wax cold.
But he that shall endure unto the end,
the same shall be saved.
And this Gospel of the Kingdom
shall be preached in all the world
for a witness unto all nations;
And then shall the end come.

– Yeshua HaMashiach

Acknowledgements

To the remnant called true and faithful Israel for whom the prophecies and the promises will be fulfilled. I encourage you to hold fast to those promises by faith while keeping the Law in earnest expectation of Messiah.

To Jon and Susan McMahon, thank you! A special thank you to Greg Isaacs and Frances Greene for their assistance in the preparation of this book.

Preface

The book of Hebrews must be included in the grouping we call "the Hebrew Epistles." In the New Testament, Hebrews is the first of the eight letters written to the Jews. They are intended for those who follow the Gospel of the Kingdom preached by the Messiah during His earthly ministry. This book focuses on the seven letters that immediately follow the book of Hebrews.

In my doctoral dissertation, I compared the structure of the New Testament to a form of Hebrew poetry called a "chiasmus." God ordained only Jewish men to record His oracles in writing.[1] Therefore, the order of the books in the New Testament could be arranged as a chiasmus. Although this structure may not have been known at the time, by the individual authors, God foreknew its final result.

---

1 Luke is the writer of his gospel and the book of Acts. He was not a Greek or Gentile as some teach. He was a Grecian Jew.

This simple poetic structure uses a balanced arrangement in its unique order:

A	The Four Gospels	Jewish
B	Acts of the Apostles	Transition
C	Pauline Epistles	Gentile
B′	Hebrews	Transition
A′	Hebrew Epistles & Revelation	Jewish

I include this only as a reference because it is broad in nature. It gives you an overall idea of how I saw the layout of the New Testament. Too many people choose bits and pieces of Scripture and try to create an interpretation. This is called inductive reasoning or "the bottom up" approach. The other approach is called "deductive reasoning" or "the top down" approach. It is this latter approach we will be using in this book.

The above concepts are best explained with a story. I bought three 1000-piece puzzles for a Men's Bible Study I was teaching. Each puzzle had a large red object in the picture such as a barn or covered bridge. I broke all the pieces up into a large wicker basket. Then, they passed it around the table and each of them was told to take twenty-five pieces. They could look at each other's piece. Then, I asked them to tell me what the picture was.

I had been at this country church for twenty years. A line of preachers had come through the door over the years. Each preacher approached the Bible using a different system of theology. The pieces they chose from the three baskets represented the bits and pieces that had in their collective beliefs. When I told them the puzzle pieces came from three different puzzles, they asked, "How are we supposed to figure this out?" I told them it was difficult seeing that two of them were missing a bunch of pieces. Only one puzzle had all the pieces and made up the correct picture completely.

I held up the cover from the puzzle box. It was the red covered bridge. This is the only complete puzzle. I asked them, "How much easier would it be if I showed you the cover picture first?" They had tried to figure out the puzzle by putting bits and pieces they had together. They were using inductive reasoning or "the bottom up" approach. They had looked at the pieces and tried to make sense of them. Since these did not have the entire picture, it was mostly guessing. (I am making an important point here.) However, once they saw the big picture, they could find the individual pieces on the cover and could begin placing them appropriately. This is "deductive reasoning" or "the top down" approach. I try to start all my students with an overall "systematic" understanding of the Bible. In this book, we will use this diagram above like the picture on the front of a puzzle box.

This system is a powerful tool you can use to interpret Scripture. I have rigorously tested this approach for ten years. All theories must be tested. I can personally testify that it works! I have written or edited commentaries for the majority of the New Testament using this approach. Again, we will use this tool to interpret these seven Hebrew epistles.

In the diagram, I called Hebrews a "transition." This is because it is the first book to follow the Pauline Epistles. Paul's letters were written to Gentiles. I believe that he was the writer of Hebrews and that he wrote it specifically to the Jews. In the commentary on Hebrews, I justify my reasons for believing this. The seven epistles which follow Hebrews were also written to Jewish believers. The final book, Revelation, is the grand finale of God's work. It ends with the complete restoration of God's Creation, the eradication of sin, the establishment of the eternal Kingdom promised to David, and the crowning of the Jesus Christ the Messiah as King.

The Bible was written "for" all believers who want to understand God and His plan. However, all the Bible was written "to" all believers. The Apostle Paul taught that all Scripture can be trusted. 2 Timothy. 3:16:

> 16 **All scripture** is given by inspiration of God, and is **profitable for doctrine, for reproof, for correction, for instruction in righteousness.**

He also gave specific instructions to Timothy, his student in training. So that Timothy would not be ashamed of misinterpreting or misunderstanding the Bible, he was instructed to partition the Word of Truth. The Greek word *orthotomeo* interpreted here as "rightly dividing" literally means "to cut with great precision." Then, and only then, can Timothy correctly understand God's Word. 2 Timothy 2:15:

> 15 **Study to shew thyself approved unto God, a workman that needeth not to be ashamed, rightly dividing the word of truth.**

This approach applies to anyone who wants to understand the Bible. This includes both Jews and Gentiles! If this is something new to you, then I suggest that you allow the proof to validate this claim.

There are four authors who wrote the seven letters. We will begin with an introduction of each of them before moving onto their writing. They are: James, Peter, John, and Jude. All of them are writing to followers of the Kingdom Gospel. Combining them into one book should not diminish, in any way, their individual importance. It is only intended for convenience – having one book for all seven of these smaller letters.

Finally, I will end the Preface with a word to Gentiles and those saved by the Gospel of Grace. Like the book of Hebrews, we cannot commandeer the contents that were intended for others. These letters were written to Jewish believers. If you try to add the Gospel of the Kingdom to the Gospel of Grace, you create something else which is not a gospel at all. For this reason, Paul warned the Galatians about doing just this. Galatians 1:6-7:

> 6 **I marvel that <u>ye are so soon removed from him that called you into the grace of Christ unto another gospel:</u> 7 Which <u>is not another;</u> but there be some that trouble you, and would pervert the gospel of Christ.**

Those saved by the Gospel of Grace are saved by grace, through faith; without works. The Gospel of the Kingdom is different. God requires true and faithful Israel to believe by faith that Jesus is their Messiah and the Son of God. Additionally, they must repent of their sins. The word "repent" means "to do an about-face or turn back" from their sins. As a public sign of their inward change, they must be baptized and continue to show proof of their faith by "doing" good works. It would be impossible to add these requirements to the Gospel of Grace. It would alter it into something else. Finally, there is one other requirement for the Jews. They must have faith and "endure unto the end" in order to be saved. Matthew 24:13:

> 13 **But he that shall endure unto the end, the same shall be saved.**

The coming Tribulation will be a time of testing for the Jews. It is called "the time of Jacob's trouble which is true and faithful Israel. Jeremiah 30:7:

> 7 **Alas! for that day is great, so that none is like it: it is even <u>the time of Jacob's trouble</u>; but he shall be saved out of it.**

True and faithful Israel will be saved! They must endure to the end and their sins will be forgiven. It is to this true and faithful remnant of Israel these epistles were written.

1

Introduction to James

The Apostle James was one of the Twelve who were chosen by the Messiah. At the beginning of Jesus' earthly ministry, Jewish men would learn and teach what the Master taught them. The word "disciple" simply means "student. It would be to these men that Jesus would entrust the good news of the Gospel of the Kingdom.

This kingdom was promised to King David whose throne would be established forever. This eternal kingdom would be ruled from Jerusalem. The Eternal King would be David's greater son. This was not Solomon, but Jesus Christ. There are multiple occasions in the gospel where the children of Israel called Jesus Christ, "Son of David," in recognition of this. The book of Matthew, the first book in the New Testament, opens with the geneaology that established Jesus' rightful claim to David's throne.

Matthew 1:1:

1 The book of the generation of <u>Jesus</u> <u>Christ, the son of David, the son of</u> <u>Abraham</u>.

The book of James was not penned by James, the son of Zebedee. James and his brother John were called "the sons of thumber." This James was killed by King Herod in Acts 12:1-2:

1 Now about that time Herod the king stretched forth his hands to vex certain of the church. 2 And he killed James the brother of John with the sword.

There was another James. This one is often referred to as the brother of Jesus. Actually, he would have been a half-brother sharing only their mother in common. The people in His hometown knew both Jesus and His family. It is this James who wrote the book we will study. Matthew 13:54-55:

54 And when he [Jesus] was come into his own country, he taught them in their synagogue, insomuch that they were astonished, and said, Whence hath this man this wisdom, and these mighty works? 55 <u>Is not this the carpenter's son?</u>

**is not his mother called Mary? and his
brethren, James, and Joses, and Simon,
and Judas?**

The Apostle Paul confirms the role of James,
the brother of Christ, at two meetings in Jerusalem.
The first is recorded in Galatians 1:18-19:

> 18 **Then after three years I went up to Je-
> rusalem to see Peter, and abode with
> him fifteen days. 19 But other of the
> apostles saw I none, save [except] James
> the Lord's brother.**

The second was at the Jerusalem Council in which all
the apostles agreed on the division of their minis-
tries. Galatians 2:9

> 9 **And when James, Cephas [Peter], and
> John, who seemed to be pillars, per-
> ceived the grace that was given unto me,
> they gave to me and Barnabas the right
> hands of fellowship; that we should go
> unto the heathen [Gentiles], and they
> unto the circumcision {Jews].**

James had become a pillar in the early Kingdom Church. Even Peter, when visiting the Apostle
Paul, was affected by James' authority. A group of

Jews were sent from Jerusalem by James to "visit" the believers in Antioch who were Gentile believers saved by grace through faith alone. Peter's change in demeanor towards this Gentile believers was observed by Paul who confronted Peter. Galatians 2:11-12:

> 11 **But when Peter was come to Antioch, I withstood him to the face, because he was to be blamed.**
>
> 12 **For before that certain came [were sent] from James, he did eat with the Gentiles: but when they were come, he withdrew and separated himself, fearing them which were of the circumcision.**

Therefore, we can reasonably assume that the book of James was indeed written by James, the Lord's half-brother. Both James and Jude were sons of Joseph and Mary. Jesus Christ and His two brothers shared the same mother, Mary. It is this James who wrote the letter that we now read.

2

James 1

As we start, I would like you to take a moment and look at the greeting. Most epistles open by identifying two things: who is sending the letter and to whom the letter is being sent. This also applies here also. James 1:1:

> 1 **James, a servant of God and of the Lord Jesus Christ, to the twelve tribes which are scattered abroad, greeting.**

Allow me to share a story to make a point. A while ago, I was teaching a weekly Men's Bible Study with an average of ten to twelve blue collar guys. I was teaching Ephesians and explaining Paul's salvation gospel of grace by faith without works. (See Ephesians 2:8-9.) One of the characters abruptly blurted out, "Hey! Wait a minute! What about what it says in

James where it says that faith without works is dead?!?" We stopped the class and looked at the verses in question which was James 2:18-26. We will get to them shortly. So, we turned to these verses and read them aloud.

He was pleased with himself that he had made his point. Then, I asked everyone to turn to the first verse in James and we also read it aloud. Here it is again.

> 1 **James, a servant of God and of the Lord Jesus Christ, <u>to the twelve tribes which are scattered abroad</u>, greeting.**

So, I asked him, "Which tribe are you from?" When we are reading from the Bible, we must know to whom the letter is being written. When a great persecution came upon them, the faithful Jews scattered into other countries. We know the coming Tribulation will be much worse from the words of Jesus in Matthew 24:21-22:

> 21 **For then shall be great tribulation, such as was not since the beginning of the world to this time, no, nor ever shall be.**

> 22 **And except those days should be**

shortened, there should no flesh be saved: but for the elect's sake those days shall be shortened.

James and these other letters will continue to provide instruction and encouragement to the Jews who wait for the arrival of the Kingdom and their King

James continues by calling them his "brethren" or "brothers" because they share in the same heritage and calling. James 1:2-4:

2 My brethren, count it all joy when ye fall into divers temptations; 3 Knowing this, that the trying of your faith worketh patience. 4 But let patience have her perfect work, that ye may be perfect and entire, wanting nothing.

He tells them that being tested by many means should be considered a joy. Why? This continual trying or testing results in the proving their faith. Eventually, it brings about patience.

The Jews who follow the Kingdom Gospel are required to continue in their faith and endure unto the end. (See Matthew 24:13.) Furthermore, they must continue to prove their faith by doing good works. It is important to note that works can never provide salvation. Salvation cannot be earned! If that were possible, then there was no purpose for the Son of God to be crucified and suffer for all. However, for Kingdom Believers, their works are proof that their faith remains alive! What does James mean by "let patience have her perfect work?" He is saying that by remaining patient during their trials and tribulations that their faith is being made perfect and, therefore, lacking nothing. Their persevering with patience is a "perfect work" and meets the requirement for proof of a living faith.

The word "upbraid" would mean "reproach or looking down upon." They are encouraged to ask God for understanding. Verse 5:

> 5 **If any of you lack wisdom, let him ask of God, that giveth to all men liberally, and upbraideth not; and it shall be given him.**

When asking God for something, there must be an expectation He will answer. They must ask in faith and hold onto that faith in anticipation of a reply. Verses 6-8:

> 6 **But let him <u>ask in faith</u>, nothing [not] wavering. For he that wavereth is like a wave of the sea driven with the wind**

and tossed.

7 For let not that man think that he shall receive any thing of the Lord. 8 A double minded man is unstable in all his ways.

Asking without having faith is being double-minded. God's relationship with His people is centered upon their faith in Him. Without faith, they will receive nothing.

From the early church period, there was a sharing of goods and belongings. Those that had gave and it was distributed to those in need. James was present when this was occurring. Paul referred to the children of Abraham as "the commonwealth of Israel." (See Eph. 2:12.) The theme of sharing in their blessings remains. Verses 9-11:

9 Let the brother of low degree rejoice in that he is exalted: 10 But the rich, in that he is made low: because as the flower of the grass he shall pass away.

11 For the sun is no sooner risen with a burning heat, but it withereth the grass, and the flower thereof falleth, and the grace of the fashion of it perisheth: so

also shall the rich man fade away in his ways.

He reminds them of the temporary nature of all men.

Speaking of temptation is trying or testing, the word "endureth" is used. The runner who endures the pain and challenge of the race is striving to win the prize. Here, their prize for enduring until the end is their salvation. This theme is not new. It remains a theme going forward since preached in the gospels. Matthew 24:13:

> 13 **But he that shall endure unto the end, the same shall be saved.**

Let us continue with James 1:12:

> 12 **Blessed is the man that endureth temptation: for when he is tried, he shall receive the crown of life, which the Lord hath promised to them that love him.**

The Jews will not receive forgiveness of sins until their Messiah returns to establish His Kingdom. Until then, their sins are held in "remission" or abeyance. (See Acts 2:38-39.) Forgiveness and eternal life have been promised to those who run and "endure unto the end." Their prize is "the crown of life."

This concept of delayed salvation for the Jews is important. The Gospel of the Kingdom is different from the Gospel of Grace. Let us look at Peter's speech to the Jews at Pentecost. Acts 2:37-39:

> 37 **Now when they heard this, they were pricked in their heart, and said unto Peter and to the rest of the apostles, Men and brethren, <u>what shall we do?</u>**
>
> 38 **Then Peter said unto them, <u>Repent, and be baptized every one of you in the name of Jesus Christ for the remission of sins</u>, and ye shall receive the gift of the Holy Ghost. 39 <u>For the promise is unto you, and to your children</u>, and to all that are afar off, even as many as the Lord our God shall call.**

The reason for delaying salvation for the Jews has a lot to do with their repeated failure to keep their faith. The Old Testament is filled with stories as evidence of this. So, their history justifies God's requirement of (1) constantly proving a living faith by their actions and (2) keeping their faith until the end.

James continues by providing information

about the progression of temptation. It is like a seed that, when germinated, brings forth a plant that yields its deadly fruit. James 1: 13-15:

> 13 **Let no man say when he is tempted, I am tempted of [by] God: for God cannot be tempted with evil, neither tempteth he any man:**
>
> 14 **But every man is tempted, when he is drawn away of [by] his own lust, and enticed.** 15 **Then when lust hath conceived, it bringeth forth sin: and sin, when it is finished, bringeth forth death.**

Paul stated a universal fact. Romans 6:23:

> 23 **For the wages of sin is death; but the gift of God is eternal life through Jesus Christ our Lord.**

The consequences of sin is death. Salvation is always a gift given by the God. This truth applies regardless of the dispensation or individual although different terms or conditions may apply.

James' states that "every good gift and every perfect gift" come from God Who is unchanging.

James 1:16-17:

> 16 **Do not err, my beloved brethren.** 17
> **Every good gift and every perfect gift is**
> **from above, and cometh down from the**
> **Father of lights, with whom is no varia-**
> **bleness, neither shadow of turning.**

There is no "variableness" or "flexibility" for treat-
ment. There is no changing of His mind. God's Word
stands unalterable. It was God Who determined that
the Jewish Believers should be the first harvest. The
word "firstfruits" is a reference to Pentecost. Pentecost is the "Festival of the Firstfruits" from the harvest.

During His earthly ministry, Jesus mentions
the "harvest," but He was referring to a harvest of
true and faithful Israel. (See Matt. 9:37,38; 13:30, 39;
Mk. 4:29; Lk. 10:2.) He is telling His hearers they
should make ready for the harvest. John 4:34-35:

> 34 **Jesus saith unto them, My meat is to**
> **do the will of him that sent me, and to**
> **finish his work.**

> 35 **Say not ye, There are yet four months,**
> **and then cometh harvest? behold, I say**
> **unto you, Lift up your eyes, and look on**

**the fields; for they are white already to
harvest.**

Picture a large field of wheat blowing in the
breeze like amber waves. Early in the harvest time,
there are certain corners or edges of the field that
ripen first. They are ready for harvest. This portion
of the harvest belongs to the Lord. It is to be an offering dedicated to God. These initial believers had
heard His message and followed His Gospel of the
Kingdom. They were the firstfruits. 1 James 18:

> 18 **Of his own will begat he us with the
> word of truth, <u>that we should be a kind
> of firstfruits of his creatures.</u>**

There are multiple references to the
"firstfruits" throughout the Old Testament. We will
limit it to only one. Deuteronomy 26:9-10:

> 9 **And he hath brought us into this place,
> and hath given us this land, even a land
> that floweth with milk and honey.**

> 10 **And now, behold, I have brought <u>the
> firstfruits</u> of the land, which thou, O
> LORD, hast given me. And thou shalt
> set it before the LORD thy God, and
> worship before the LORD thy God:**

The concept of "firstfruits" belonging to the LORD stems to the Promised Land. It was promised to the Seed of Israel as was the promise of the Kingdom through King David's Seed. As a note, the word "Seed" used in these promises is singular and not plural. You might want to stop and think about that.

James encouraged moderation in their temperament as they interact with each other. Becoming upset or angry with each other is contrary to the righteous intent of God. James 1:19-20:

> 19 **Wherefore, my beloved brethren, let every man be swift to hear, slow to speak, slow to wrath:** 20 **For the wrath of man worketh not the righteousness of God.**

That is good advice for everyone. Be quick to listen, slow to speak, and slow to get angry.

The word "superfluity" means "the quality or condition of being overabundant or excessive." Verse 21:

> 21 **Wherefore lay [set] apart all filthiness and superfluity of naughtiness, and receive with meekness the engrafted word, which is able to save your souls.**

The last portion of this requires some explanation. The word "grafted" is the same as having completed the "process of grafting" as into another tree. Something from one tree is inserted into or grafted into another tree. If Jesus Christ is the olive tree, then dead branches could be removed and others grafted in.

Paul writes to the Gentile believers in Rome explaining to them the current status of Israel. In Romans 11, he uses the analogy of true Israel being an olive tree. Those who departed from the faith, being called a wild olive tree, can be "grafted" back into the cultivated olive tree. See *Romans: Dispensationally Considered* for a detailed explanation. Unbelieving Israel is the branches that will be broken off and thrown into the fire. The Apostle John records a similar analogy of Christ in which He is the vine. Sometimes we need to be reminded that the four gospels, Hebrews, and the seven Hebrew epistles carry the same message. John 15:1-6:

> 1 **I am the true vine, and my Father is the husbandman. 2 Every branch in me that beareth not fruit he taketh away: and every branch that beareth fruit, he purgeth [prunes] it, that it may bring forth more fruit.**
>
> 3 **Now ye are clean through the word**

which I have spoken unto you. 4 Abide in me, and I in you. As the branch cannot bear fruit of itself, except it abide in the vine; no more can ye, except ye abide in me.

5 I am the vine, ye are the branches: He that abideth in me, and I in him, the same bringeth forth much fruit: for without me ye can do nothing.

6 If a man abide not in me, he is cast forth as a branch, and is withered; and men gather them, and cast them into the fire, and they are burned.

True and faithful Israel must hear the Word of God, keep it hidden in their hearts, and also put it into action. According to the Gospel of the Kingdom, believers have the requirement of works, not to save them, but to substantiate their faith. James 1:22-24:

22 But be ye doers of the word, and not hearers only, deceiving your own selves. 23 For if any be a hearer of the word, and not a doer, he is like unto a man beholding his natural face in a glass [mirror]:

24 For he beholdeth himself, and goeth his way, and straightway forgetteth what manner of man he was.

They must study the Law and continue to do what is required of them in their lives. Verse 25:

25 But whoso looketh into the perfect law of liberty, and continueth therein, he being not a forgetful hearer, but a doer of the work, this man shall be blessed in his deed.

God will bless the believer who keeps the faith and does the work. He knows those who are fakes by giving lip service, but doing nothing. They are only deceiving themselves. Verse 26:

26 If any man among you seem to be religious, and bridleth not his tongue, but deceiveth his own heart, this man's religion is vain.

God knows the true and faithful Israel by their actions. Contrariwise, for those saved by grace through faith, they are saved by faith alone. They need no works as proof of their righteousness. They believed and have the righteousness of Christ. For Kingdom Believers, that is not the case. They must

show works of faith, remain free from sin, and endure to the end. Verse 27:

**27 Pure religion and undefiled before
God and the Father is this, To visit the
fatherless and widows in their affliction, and to keep himself unspotted
from the world.**

3

James 2

At the beginning of the Kingdom Church, there was sharing of property among the brethren. It was a commonwealth and everyone shared so that no one would be in want. Paul referred to the Jews as "the commonwealth of Israel" in Ephesians 2:12. Luke paints a picture of the early years of the Kingdom Church in Acts 2:42-47:

> 42 **And they continued stedfastly in the apostles' doctrine and fellowship, and in breaking of bread, and in prayers.**
>
> 43 **And fear came upon every soul: and many wonders and signs were done by the apostles.**
>
> 44 **And all that believed were together,**

and had all things common; 45 And sold their possessions and goods, and parted them to all men, as every man had need.

46 And they, continuing daily with one accord in the temple, and breaking bread from house to house, did eat their meat with gladness and singleness of heart, 47 Praising God, and having favour with all the people. And the Lord added to the church daily such as should be saved.

Did you notice that these new believers met daily in the Temple? This makes it clear that all the members were Jews since no Gentiles were allowed in the Temple.

James, writing to these Kingdom Believers, continues. James 2:1:

1 My brethren, have not the faith of our Lord Jesus Christ, the Lord of glory, with respect of persons.

There must be no differentiation among believers and no showing of partiality. Verses 2-4:

2 For if there come unto your assembly

a man with a gold ring, in goodly apparel, and there come in also a poor man in vile raiment;

3 And ye have respect to him that weareth the gay clothing, and say unto him, Sit thou here in a good place; and say to the poor, Stand thou there, or sit here under my footstool:

4 Are ye not then partial in yourselves, and are become judges of evil thoughts?

Anything causing attention to be drawn to oneself makes it about ego and not humility. For God's Son humbled Himself and became a Servant. This is consistent with what Christ taught during His earthly ministry to the Jews. Matthew 23:11-12:

11 But he that is greatest among you shall be your servant.

12 And whosoever shall exalt himself shall be abased; and he that shall humble himself shall be exalted.

Like a good preacher, he urges them to listen to what he is saying and pay attention. What he is teaching them is an important part of the Kingdom

Gospel. Verse 5:

> 5 **Hearken, my beloved brethren, Hath not God chosen the poor of this world rich in faith, and heirs of the kingdom which he hath promised to them that love him?**

They must be careful not to act in the same manner as the rich. Their arrogance and pride is seen, even blaspheming the name of Jesus. Verses 6-7:

> 6 **But ye have despised the poor. Do not rich men oppress you, and draw [take] you before the judgment seats?**

> 7 **Do not they blaspheme that worthy name by the which ye are called?**

One of the Pharisees asked Jesus a question, "Master, which is the great commandment in the law?" (Matt. 22:36). His response is found in Matthew 22:37-40:

> 37 **Jesus said unto him, Thou shalt love the Lord thy God with all thy heart, and with all thy soul, and with all thy mind.**

38 This is the first and great commandment. 39 And the second is like unto it, Thou shalt love thy neighbour as thyself.

40 On these two commandments hang all the law and the prophets.

So, nothing has changed. The message to "the lost sheep of Israel" remains the same. (See Matt. 10:6; 15:24.)

He continues with this thought. James 2:8:

8 If ye fulfil the royal law according to the scripture, Thou shalt love thy neighbour as thyself, ye do well:

Below, the word "convinced" means "persuaded in mind, satisfied with the evidence, or convicted by truth." Verses 9-10:

9 But if ye have respect to persons, ye commit sin, and are convinced of [by] the law as transgressors.

10 For whosoever shall keep the whole law, and yet offend in one point, he is guilty of all.

This last verse is very important to understand. The Law of Moses is a binding covenant and it is still in effect today. When the Jews accepted this agreement, they were bound to the Law in its entirety. In other words, by breaking only one point of the Law, it meant they were breaking the entire agreement.

James makes this point clear in verse 11:

11 For he that said, Do not commit adultery, said also, Do not kill. Now if thou commit no adultery, yet if thou kill, thou art become a transgressor of the law.

Again, the Mosaic Covenant is an agreement between God and the children of Israel. Verses 12-13:

12 So speak ye, and so do, as they that shall be judged by the law of liberty.

13 For he shall have judgment without mercy, that hath shewed no mercy; and mercy rejoiceth against judgment.

The Prophet Hosea wrote these words of God, "For I desired mercy, and not sacrifice; and the knowledge of God more than burnt offerings" (Hos. 6:6). Jesus shared this with the Jews during His earthly ministry. (See Matt. 9:13, 12:7.) Mercy does rejoice when it triumphs over judgment. He warns that this will not happen for those who do not show mercy themselves.

We have arrived at a verse familiar to many Christians who try to incorporate these verses into their own gospel. However, when this is done, it fails. Why? First, it fails because the Gospel of the Kingdom is different from the Gospel of Grace. Second, the Gospel of the Kingdom as delivered by Christ and the Twelve, is sent exclusively to the "circumcision" – the children of Israel. (See Gal. 2:7-9.) The Jews are promised salvation when their Messiah returns to establish His Kingdom. They must continue to keep the Law. Since Israel's history continually showed a lack of faith throughout the Old Testament, they must continue to demonstrate their faith is active. How are they to do this? They do it by their actions or works until His return. See Jesus' words in Matthew 24:13:

13 **But <u>he that shall endure unto the end,
the same shall be saved.</u>**

Now, it makes sense that James gives instructions concerning works or actions. They are necessary as proof of their living faith. James 2:14-18:

14 What doth it profit, my brethren, though a man say he hath faith, and have not works? can faith save him?

15 If a brother or sister be naked, and destitute of daily food, **16** And one of you say unto them, Depart in peace, be ye warmed and filled; notwithstanding ye give them not those things which are needful to the body; what doth it profit? **17** Even so faith, if it hath not works, is dead, being alone.

18 Yea, a man may say, Thou hast faith, and I have works: shew me thy faith without thy works, and I will shew thee my faith by my works.

How many try to share their faith with others only to be told by others that they believe in God? Somehow they think that believing there is a God is enough. Satan knows there is a God and has appeared before Him. However, that is not enough. Verse 19:

19 Thou believest that there is one God; thou doest well: the devils also believe, and tremble.

James asks these Jews a question. Verse 20:

> **20 But wilt thou know, O vain man, that faith without works is dead?**

He cites examples from Israel's history beginning with Abraham. He shows that faith must be accompanied by works or actions. Verses 21-24:

> **21 Was not Abraham our father justified by works, when he had offered Isaac his son upon the altar? 22 Seest thou how faith wrought with his works, and by works was faith made perfect?**

> **23 And the scripture was fulfilled which saith, Abraham believed God, and it was imputed unto him for righteousness: and he was called the Friend of God. 24 Ye see then how that by works a man is justified, and not by faith only.**

Abraham was the patriarch and father of the children of Israel. Yet, Rahab was a lowly person. She exercised faith in her service to God's people. Her faith was evident in her actions. Verse 25:

> **25 Likewise also was not Rahab the harlot justified by works, when she had**

received the messengers, and had sent them out another way?

James concludes this chapter with an important point. For the Jews following the Gospel of the Kingdom, they must remember that "faith without works is dead." Verse 26:

26 **For as the body without the spirit is dead, so faith without works is dead also.**

4

James 3

This group of Kingdom Believers were called "the Way." When they became more known by the people, they were looked at as being different. The word "master" means "someone who directs, governs or rules over others." James cautions them not to offend others by what they say or do. James 3:1-2:

> 1 **My brethren, be not many masters, knowing that we shall receive the greater condemnation.**
>
> 2 **For in many things we offend all. If any man offend not in word, the same is a perfect man, and able also to bridle [control] the whole body.**

If they are able to bridle or control their speech, they

will accomplished what is expected of them.

He continues by addressing the difficulties of some believers in controlling their speech. He calls the "tongue" a powerful force. Verses 3-5.

> 3 **Behold, we put bits in the horses' mouths, that they may obey us; and we turn about their whole body.**
>
> 4 **Behold also the ships, which though they be so great, and are driven of fierce winds, yet are they turned about with a very small helm, whithersoever the governor listeth.**
>
> 5 **Even so the tongue is a little member, and boasteth great things. Behold, how great a matter a little fire kindleth!**

The tongue has great influence over the direction of our actions. Once we say speak our mind, our thoughts are fixed in the minds of others. If we withhold our tongue, then we can still think what we want. By keeping it to ourselves, others are none the wiser.

He continues with verses 6-8:

6 And the tongue is a fire, a world of iniquity: so is the tongue among our members, that it defileth the whole body, and setteth on fire the course of nature; and it is set on fire of hell.

7 For every kind of beasts, and of birds, and of serpents, and of things in the sea, is tamed, and hath been tamed of [by] mankind: 8 But the tongue can no man tame; it is an unruly evil, full of deadly poison.

The tongue can be a terrible thing. It can at one moment praise God and, in another, curse men. Verses 9-12:

9 Therewith [By it] bless we God, even the Father; and therewith [by it] curse we men, which are made after the similitude of God. 10 Out of the same mouth proceedeth [both] blessing and cursing. My brethren, these things ought not so to be.

11 Doth [Does] a fountain send forth at the same place sweet water and bitter?

12 Can the fig tree, my brethren, bear ol-

ive berries? either a vine, figs? so can no
fountain both yield salt water and fresh.

James brings this to a conclusion by asking the
Kingdom Believers a question. The word "endued"
means "provided with a particular quality or ability." The word "conversation" means "manner of living." Verses 13-14:

13 **Who is a wise man and endued
[blessed] with knowledge among you?
let him shew out of a good conversation
[manner of living] his works with
meekness of [by] wisdom.**

14 **But if ye have bitter envying and
strife in your hearts, glory not, and lie
not against the truth.**

Bitter envying and strife is not received from
God. It form of wisdom is, in fact, just the opposite.
Verses 15-16:

15 **This wisdom descendeth not from
above, but is earthly, sensual, devilish.**

16 **For where envying and strife is, there
is confusion and every evil work.**

34

However, the wisdom from above is from God. He lists the attributes of Godly wisdom in verses 17-18:

> 17 **But the wisdom that is from above is first pure, then peaceable, gentle, and easy to be intreated, full of mercy and good fruits, without partiality, and without hypocrisy.**
>
> 18 **And the fruit of righteousness is sown in peace of them that make peace.**

5

James 4

In this chapter, James begins with an interesting statement. It concerns the cause of wars. Wars are caused by people "lusting after" that which they do not have, but want. This applies to disagreements within the assembly as well. James 4:1-2:

> 1 **From whence come wars and fightings among you? come they not hence, even [that is to say] of your lusts that war in your members?**
>
> 2 **Ye lust, and have not: ye kill, and desire to have, and cannot obtain: ye fight and war, yet ye have not, because ye ask not.**

They have not because they do not ask God. Instead, they take it upon themselves to obtain what they desire by their own means. Verses 3-5:

> **3 Ye ask, and receive not, because ye ask amiss, that ye may consume it upon your lusts.**
>
> **4 Ye adulterers and adulteresses, know ye not that the friendship of the world is enmity with God? whosoever therefore will be a friend of the world is the enemy of God.**
>
> **5 Do ye think that the scripture saith in vain, The spirit that dwelleth in us lusteth to envy?**

He is speaking about the human spirit. His questions are intended to make them think and consider what Scripture teaches. They must not do what is contrary to God's Word.

The proud and haughty people are determined to achieve, to accomplish, or to attain what they want. They do this contrary to what God wants His people to be. He wants them to depend upon Him. God's people are to be humble and come to Him with their requests. Like He did in the Wilderness, He wants to provide for their daily needs. Jesus gave them a model prayer we call the Lord's Prayer. Saying, "give us this day our daily bread." Saying, in other words, "God, meet our daily needs." Christ taught the Kingdom Believers to be dependent upon God; not to be independent. Self-pride comes from self-dependence while humility comes from dependence upon Him. Verse 6:

> 6 But he giveth more grace. Wherefore he saith, God resisteth the proud, but giveth grace unto the humble.

He continues with instructions on how they are to achieve this. Verses 7-10:

> 7 <u>Submit yourselves therefore to God</u>. Resist the devil, and he will flee from you. 8 Draw nigh to God, and he will draw nigh to you. Cleanse your hands, ye sinners; and purify your hearts, ye double minded.

> 9 Be afflicted, and mourn, and weep: let your laughter be turned to mourning, and your joy to heaviness. 10 <u>Humble yourselves in the sight of the Lord, and he shall lift you up</u>.

Humility comes at a cost of overcoming pride which

means focusing more on God and less on self. All good things are received from the hand of God.

James now addresses the way they are to interact with fellow believers. Putting aside selfish pride, they are not to judge one other. There is only one truly righteous Judge. Verses 11-12:

> 11 Speak not evil one of another, brethren. He that speaketh evil of his brother, and judgeth his brother, speaketh evil of the law, and judgeth the law: but if thou judge the law, thou art not a doer of the law, but a judge.
>
> 12 There is one lawgiver, who is able to save and to destroy: who art thou that judgest another?

Nothing has changed from the message delivered by Jesus and His Twelve to "the lost sheep of Israel" during His earthly ministry. I would recommend you stop for a moment. Read what many refer to as "the Beatitudes" found in Matthew 5:1-12. Can you see the similarities of the Beatitudes in James' letter?

Everyone thinks that they have control over their lives. When, in fact, they are totally dependent upon God whether they admit it or not. James teaches this in verses 13-16:

> 13 **Go to now, ye that say, Today or to-morrow we will go into such a city, and continue there a year, and buy and sell, and get gain:**
>
> 14 **Whereas ye know not what shall be on the morrow. <u>For what is your life? It is even a vapour, that appeareth for a little time, and then vanisheth away</u>.**
>
> 15 **For that ye ought to say, If the Lord will, we shall live, and do this, or that.** 16 **But now ye rejoice in your boastings: all such rejoicing is evil.**

All men fall into this error. It is part of that "self-nature" we got from our Adam's original sin. Knowing good and evil we, like Satan, have the pride of life and want to be our own god. Who are we to say what will and will not happen? God is the only one Who knows all the circumstances. Believers must understand this. Everything, repeat everything, is at the will and pleasure of God. Kingdom Believers must remain dependent upon their King!

James concludes with this. Kingdom Believers have one singular responsibility. They are to know

God's will and to do it; otherwise, they are sinners. Verse 17:

17 Therefore to him that knoweth to do good, and doeth it not, to him it is sin.

6

James 5

In the four gospels, Jesus had a lot to say about the wealthy – those whose wealth was obtained through vanity of selfish pride. This is exemplified in His words, "For it is easier for a camel to go through a needle's eye, than for a rich man to enter into the kingdom of God" (Lk. 18:25). We start with James 5:1-3:

> 1 **Go to now, ye rich men, weep and howl for your miseries that shall come upon you. 2 Your riches are corrupted, and your garments are motheaten.**
>
> 3 **Your gold and silver is cankered; and the rust of them shall be a witness against you, and shall eat your flesh as it were fire. Ye have heaped treasure to-**

gether for the last days.

The phrase "last days" refer to the time of judgment that is coming. These are the last seven years called the Tribulation. Jesus predicts them in Matthew 24.

James continues about the wealthy who have obtained their wealth corruptly. He refers to laborers who have done the work of harvesting the wealthy man's fields. Then, he withheld the wages from those who labored. Verse 4:

> 4 Behold, the hire [wages] of the labourers who have reaped down your fields, which is of you kept back by fraud, [they] crieth: and the cries of them which have reaped are entered into the ears of the Lord of sabaoth {Sabbath].

God hears their cries for justice. The judgment of the wicked is coming. Verse 5:

> 5 Ye have lived in pleasure on the earth, and been wanton; ye have nourished your hearts, as in a day of slaughter.

Additionally, because of their power and position, the wicked have committed injury to the just who does not resist them. Verse 6:

6 Ye have condemned and killed the just; and he doth not resist you.

James tells them there is consolation. He assures them that the return of the Messiah is getting closer. Verses 7-8:

7 Be patient therefore, brethren, unto the coming of the Lord. Behold, the husbandman waiteth for the precious fruit of the earth, and hath long patience for it, until he receive the early and latter rain.

8 Be ye also patient; stablish your hearts: for the coming of the Lord draweth nigh.

For the Kingdom Believers, there are only those inside and those outside. James turns his attention to those inside – fellow believers who he collectively calls "brethren." Verses 9-10:

9 Grudge not one against another, brethren, lest ye be condemned: behold, the judge standeth before the door.

10 Take, my brethren, the prophets, who have spoken in the name of the Lord,

for an example of suffering affliction, and of patience.

They are to take the prophets of Israel to be their examples. God's people have always suffered and affliction. However, they kept their faith with patience and long-suffering.

The prophets are not the only ones who are examples for them. He speaks about Job who also believed God. Verse 11:

11 **Behold, we count them [the prophets] happy which endure. Ye have heard of the patience of Job, and have seen the end of the Lord; that the Lord is very pitiful, and of tender mercy.**

The story of Job recounts all of his sufferings, but Job "have seen in the end." The Lord had pity on Job and showed him "tender mercy." The Kingdom Believers are to do likewise.

These believers must remember their human frailty. All men are made by God. It was not man who made himself. This fact of Who made them along with God's desire for them to be dependent upon Him are important. Verse 12:

12 But above all things, my brethren, swear not, neither by heaven, neither by the earth, neither by any other oath: but let your yea be yea; and your nay, nay; lest ye fall into condemnation.

All of this is tied into the message that Jesus preached to the children of Abraham – the lost sheep of Israel.

Consider these words of Jesus and compare them with James' message. Jesus is their life. Compare this with those who do not remain in Him. John 15:1-8:

1 I am the true vine, and my Father is the husbandman. 2 Every branch in me that beareth not fruit he taketh away: and every branch that beareth fruit, he purgeth [prunes] it, that it may bring forth more fruit.

3 Now ye are clean through the word which I have spoken unto you. 4 Abide in me, and I in you. As the branch cannot bear fruit of itself, except it abide in the vine; no more can ye, except ye abide in me.

5 I am the vine, ye are the branches: He that abideth in me, and I in him, the same bringeth forth much fruit: for without me ye can do nothing.

6 If a man abide not in me, he is cast forth as a branch, and is withered; and men gather them, and cast them into the fire, and they are burned.

7 If ye abide in me, and my words abide in you, ye shall ask what ye will, and it shall be done unto you. 8 Herein is my Father glorified, that ye bear much fruit; so shall ye be my disciples.

Continuing with this theme of dependency, James talks about the care of the believers. Verse 13-15:

13 Is any among you afflicted? let him pray. Is any merry? let him sing psalms. 14 Is any sick among you? let him call for the elders of the church; and let them pray over him, anointing him with oil in the name of the Lord:

15 And the prayer of faith shall save the sick, and the Lord shall raise him up;

and if he have committed sins, they shall be forgiven him.

Finally, confessing their faults to each other is a great way to reduce sin. Verse 16:

> 16 **Confess your faults one to another, and pray one for another, that ye may be healed. The effectual fervent prayer of a righteous man availeth much.**

All of God's people were human and, as such, they have their own human frailties. He gives the example of Elijah. This story begins in 1 Kings 17:1. Elijah was like all men. He was sinful, however, he did have faith. For this reason, James said, "The effectual fervent prayer of a righteous man availeth much." James finds the example of a "righteous man" in Elijah. Verse 17-18:

> 17 **Elias [Elijah] was a man subject to like passions as we are, and he prayed earnestly that it might not rain: and it rained not on the earth by the space of three years and six months.**

> 18 **And he prayed again, and the heaven gave rain, and the earth brought forth her fruit.**

If you want other examples of great people of faith in Jewish history, consider reading Hebrews 11. It is called the hall of fame for those of faith for a reason. These were all ordinary people with extraordinary faith in God. There in was the difference.

Some of the believers will stray from the truth. To do so, it is a sin for they are missing the mark. Should another believer turn them back from their error, they shall save the soul of the fallen brother and gain for themself a multitude of forgiveness. Verses 19-20:

> 19 **Brethren, if any of you do err from the truth, and one convert him;**
>
> 20 **Let him know, that he which con-verteth the sinner from the error of his way shall save a soul from death, and shall hide a multitude of sins.**

The one who returns the fallen believer to fellowship proves his own faith. And, it is this faith that covers "a multitude of sins."

This all may sound overwhelming. However, if the Kingdom Believers remember this, then they will meet all the requirements of the Law. Matthew 22:37-40:

37 Jesus said unto him, <u>Thou shalt love the Lord thy God with all thy heart, and with all thy soul, and with all thy mind.</u>

38 This is the first and great commandment. 39 And the second is like unto it, <u>Thou shalt love thy neighbour as thyself.</u>

40 <u>On these two commandments hang all the law and the prophets.</u>

7

Introduction to Peter

Peter was one of the first to be chosen and perhaps the most well-known of the Twelve. He introduced to Jesus through his brother, Andrew. John 1:40-41:

40 One of the two [men] which heard John speak, and followed him, was Andrew, Simon Peter's brother.

41 He first findeth his own brother Simon, and saith unto him, We have found the Messias, which is, being interpreted, the Christ.

Every group needs an anchor, someone whose temperament solidifies its members. This would be Peter. In their first meeting, Jesus recognized this.

Verse 42:

> 42 And he brought him to Jesus. And when Jesus beheld him, he said, Thou art Simon the son of Jona: thou shalt be called Cephas, which is by interpretation, [Petros] a stone.

Later, we see this title used again but in a different way. Much speculation was swirling amongst the people as to Who this Jesus was? When He had His disciples alone, He asked them a question. Matthew 16:15-18:

> 15 He saith unto them, But whom say ye that I am? 16 And Simon Peter answered and said, <u>Thou art the Christ, the Son of the living God.</u>

> 17 And Jesus answered and said unto him, Blessed art thou, Simon Barjona: for flesh and blood hath not revealed it unto thee, but my Father which is in heaven.

Speaking specifically to Peter about what he had just proclaimed, Jesus continues. Verse 18:

> 18 And I say also unto thee, That thou art

Peter, and <u>upon this rock I will build my church</u>; and the gates of hell shall not prevail against it.

The original New Testament was written in Greek. Here is something most people do not know. The basis for Peter's name is "petros" which is the masculine form for the word "stone" or "rock." However, the word chosen for "rock," in verse 18, was "petra" which is the feminine form of the same noun. So, why is there a difference?[2]

This technical difference is important. It has become the basis for an entire religion. (I point no fingers. My job is not to judge anyone. Like an insurance agent reading the policy, I can only tell you what the policy says. If you disagree, then take it up with a higher power.) Peter's name comes from the word "petros" which is a physical object such as a stone. When the feminine form is used, it represents something intangible like an "idea or concept" such as a "theological foundation." That is exactly the case here. The basis for the Jews' salvation is their belief in the truth of Who Jesus is. "Thou art the Christ, the Son of the living God" (Matt. 16:15). You will find

[2] George Ricker Berry, The Interlinear KJV Parallel New Testament In Greek And English Based On The Majority Text With Lexicon And Synonyms. (Grand Rapids, Mich.: Zondervan Publishing House, 1897).

this also made clear in the Hebrew epistles. This statement from Peter was revealed to him by the Father in heaven. It is the "foundation" or "petra" of the Jew's faith.

In the Preface, we discussed the system being used to interpret these letters. It is the dispensational approach. There are two books published by Grace-Word Publishing that go into great detail explaining this approach. For the Gentiles, it is *Letters To Theophilus*. For the Jews, it is *The Glorious Destiny of Israel*. There is a point in the New Testament where the Twelve Apostles meet with the Apostle Paul. The results of this meeting make clear the different between the Gospel of the Kingdom sent to the Jews and the Gospel of Grace sent to the Gentiles. Let us take a look at the evidence.

The details of the meeting was recorded in Galatians 2. It had been fourteen years since Paul had traveled to Jerusalem to see the apostles there. This second time he brought Barnabas and Titus with him. During Paul's speech in which he presented the Gospel of Grace, the others listened. His purpose was to prevent the Gospel of Grace from becoming altered or merged with the Gospel of the Kingdom. Below, the word "circumcision" refers to those under the Abrahamic Covenant for the Jews. The words "uncircumcision" or "heathen" refer to the Gentiles. Galatians 2:6-9:

> 6 But of these who seemed to be somewhat, (whatsoever they were, it maketh no matter to me: God accepteth no man's person:) for they who seemed to be somewhat in conference added nothing to me:

> 7 But contrariwise, when <u>they saw that the gospel of the uncircumcision was committed unto me, as the gospel of the circumcision was unto Peter;</u> 8 (For he that wrought effectually in Peter to the apostleship of the circumcision, the same was mighty in me toward the Gentiles:)

> 9 And when James, Cephas, and John, who seemed to be pillars, perceived the grace that was given unto me, they gave to me and Barnabas the right hands of fellowship; that we should go unto the heathen, and they unto the circumcision.

Repetition is the mother of learning and, although I wrote this information in the Preface, it is important to clearly state it again. Peter was commissioned to the Gospel of the Kingdom to be taken to the lost sheep of Israel.

Peter wrote his instructions or teaching specifically to the "circumcision." In his first epistle, he addressed those Jewish believers who were dispersed over five regions: Pontus, Galatia, Cappadocia, Asia, and Bithynia. Towards the end of his life, he wrote his second epistle. By then, it was the custom for recipients of apostolic letters to make copies and share them with other assemblies. Historical tradition has Peter dying in Rome under Emperor Nero's reign. Since he makes no mention of the destruction of Jerusalem in 70 A.D., the date of his death is generally accepted to be between 64 and 68 A.D.

Now, with this background, we can begin Peter's first epistle.

8

1 Peter 1

The dispersion of Jews leaving Jerusalem and their homeland is often called "the diaspora." These "seeds" of Israel were scattered among the nations. We saw this in James' salutation, "to the twelve tribes which are scattered abroad" (Jas. 1:1). Great persecution against those who followed the Kingdom Gospel forced them to seek safety elsewhere. This persecution came from both Rome and unbelieving Jews who did not follow Jesus Christ. In Peter's salutation, he uses the word "strangers." They were strangers in foreign lands away from their homeland which was Israel. 1 Peter 1:1:

> 1 **Peter, an apostle of Jesus Christ, to the strangers scattered throughout Pontus, Galatia, Cappadocia, Asia, and**

Bithynia,

In his salutation, he used the word "elect" as a noun. It means those "chosen or set apart by choice." It was God Who chose them from the beginning through Abraham. Verse 2:

2 **Elect according to the foreknowledge of God the Father, through sanctification of the Spirit, unto obedience and sprinkling of the blood of Jesus Christ: Grace unto you, and peace, be multiplied.**

We know that Kingdom Believers choose to believe that Jesus is both the Messiah and the Son of God. By faith, they keep the Law, do good works as proof of that faith, and must endure unto the end. What end?

In Matthew 24, the entire chapter is devoted to providing information concerning "the end." Privately, Jesus' disciples said, "Tell us, when shall these things be? and what shall be the sign of thy coming, and of the end of the world?" (Matt. 24:3). He is having this conversation with His Twelve less than one week before His Crucifixion. Notice that His comments are in regards to the "elect" in the following two references.

Matthew 24:24:

> **24 For there shall arise false Christs, and false prophets, and shall shew great signs and wonders; insomuch that, if it were possible, <u>they shall deceive the very elect.</u>**

Matthew 24:31:

> **31 And he shall send his angels with a great sound of a trumpet, and <u>they shall gather together his elect from the four winds, from one end of heaven to the other.</u>**

These elect cannot be confused with any other group as they are destined to go through the Tribulation. In the end, Jesus promises that God will gather them together again into the Promised Land.

In this same chapter, He mentioned that the "elect" who are the true and faithful Israel must endure to the end of the seven years of testing. Matthew 24:13-14:

> **13 <u>But he that shall endure unto the end, the same shall be saved.</u>**

14 And <u>this gospel of the kingdom shall be preached in all the world</u> for a witness unto all nations; and then shall the end come.

One final verse to examine outside out text is from the Prophet Jeremiah. God knew that the rulers of Israel would reject and kill their Messiah. The phrase "that great day" refers to "the final seven years." God will test or try the faith of true and faithful believers who He calls "Jacob" below. Jeremiah 30:7:

> **7** Alas! for <u>that day is great</u>, so that none is like it: it is even [that is to say] the time of Jacob's trouble; but <u>he shall be saved out of it</u>.

James, Peter, John, and Jude are writing to the Kingdom Believers who are destined to go through the Tribulation. Their writings teach and encourage those who must "endure unto the end" to be saved.

Jesus Christ, the Messiah for the Jews was raised from the dead. He is often called the "firstborn" because He was the first born from the dead. The reason for the Jews' hope of resurrection is because of Jesus Christ. In the following, Peter refers to this as a "lively hope." God wants their faith to be active. He wants their faith to be a "living hope." 1 Peter 1:3:

> **3 Blessed be the God and Father of our Lord Jesus Christ, which according to his abundant mercy hath begotten us again unto <u>a lively hope</u> by the resurrection of Jesus Christ from the dead,**

What is their hope? Their sins will be forgiven by the Messiah upon His return and salvation will be granted. This is wonderful news, but there is far more!

Believing Jews or "true Israel" were promised that an eternal Kingdom will be established by King David's Son. In the gospels, you may recall that Jesus was called "Son of David." It was for that reason. The Jews' inheritance is earthly. It is currently waiting for them in heaven. I cannot contain myself and must show you one more biblical reference concerning this future event. The Apostle John recorded what he saw in heaven in the book of Revelation. Here is what he wrote Revelation 21:2-3:

> **2 And I John saw <u>the holy city, new Jerusalem</u>, coming down from God out of heaven, prepared as a bride adorned for her husband.**

3 And I heard a great voice out of heaven saying, Behold, <u>the tabernacle of God is with men</u>, and <u>he will dwell with them, and they shall be his people</u>, and <u>God himself shall be with them, and be their God</u>.

Now, we are ready to move onto our next verse. 1 Peter 1:4-5:

4 To an <u>inheritance incorruptible, and undefiled</u>, and that fadeth not away, <u>reserved in heaven for you</u>,

5 [You] Who are <u>kept by the power of God through faith unto salvation</u> ready to be revealed in the last time.

These wonderful promises are meant to inspire and encourage them to "endure unto the end." Peter offers these instructions. Verses 6-7:

6 Wherein ye greatly rejoice, though now for a season, if need be, ye are in heaviness through manifold temptations:

7 <u>That the trial of your faith</u>, being much more precious than of gold that perish-

**eth, though it be tried with fire, <u>might
be found unto praise and honour and
glory at the appearing of Jesus Christ</u>:**

The "appearing of Jesus Christ" refers to His Second
Coming. Although they cannot presently see Him,
they still believe. They have faith in His Word that
all He has promised will happen. Verses 8-9:

> **8 Whom having not seen, ye love; in
> whom, though now ye see him not, yet
> believing, ye rejoice with joy unspeak-
> able and full of glory:**
>
> **9 Receiving the end of your faith, even
> [that is to say] the salvation of your
> souls.**

Notice that the ultimate promise to the Jews who
continue in faith is "the salvation for your souls."

The testimony of the prophets support this.
Verse 10:

> **10 Of which salvation the prophets have
> enquired and searched diligently, who
> prophesied of the grace that should
> come unto you:**

One could argue that their salvation is payment for their faith and continued works. This is not true. The word "grace" means "gift." The testing or trying is to find true Israel. It is to reveal those who have faith and their actions prove it. Why then must the Jews have their faith tested? Why will only those who keep their faith until the end be saved? God has great plans for Israel as we will see in the next chapter. Their long history of not believing God, including the crucifixion of their Messiah, justifies God's requirement for faithful Israel to continually demonstrate their faith until the end.

Isaiah was only one prophet who wrote about the sufferings of Christ. He did this approximately 700 years before His birth. (See Isaiah 52:13-53:12.) Verse 11:

> 11 **Searching what, or what manner of time the Spirit of Christ which was in them did signify, when it testified beforehand [of] the sufferings of Christ, and the glory that should follow.**

Nothing surprises God. He knew in advance that Israel would fail. At some point before His Return, Israel will realizes that they need God's Son to do for them what they could not do for themselves.

God revealed to the prophets through the Holy Spirit things they did not fully understand. Think about this. Even His disciples did not fully understand until later. Look at what Peter says following his statement of faith concerning Who Jesus is. Mark 8:29-33

29 **And he saith unto them, But whom say ye that I am? And Peter answereth and saith unto him, Thou art the Christ. 30 And he charged them that they should tell no man of him.**

31 **And he began to teach them, that the Son of man must suffer many things, and be rejected of the elders, and of the chief priests, and scribes, and be killed, and after three days rise again.**

32 <u>**And he spake that saying openly. And Peter took him [Christ], and began to rebuke him.**</u>

33 **But when he had turned about and looked on his disciples, he rebuked Peter, saying, Get thee behind me, Satan: for thou savourest not the things that be of God, but the things that be of men.**

The disciples were dumbfounded when His crucifixion took place. They scattered. Additionally, the principalities, powers and rulers of darkness did not understand. The Apostle Paul called them "princes" when he wrote, "Which none of the princes of this world knew: for had they known it, they would not have crucified the Lord of glory" (1 Cor. 2:8).

That which was not understood then, is now understood. It is the Holy Spirit Who illuminates human minds to understand the Word of God. 1 Peter 1:12:

> 12 **Unto whom it was revealed, that not unto themselves, but unto us they did minister the things, which are now reported unto you by them that have preached the gospel unto you with the Holy Ghost sent down from heaven; which things the angels desire to look into.**

These believers now have this knowledge and no one should be able to take it from them. To "gird up your loins" would be similar to saying "stand your ground." To "be sober" means "to be of sound mind." They should not be confused by anyone, but instead trust solely on the Word of God. The enemy wants Israel to be defeated. True and faithful Israel stands in the enemy's way. Verse 13:

13 Wherefore <u>gird up the loins of your mind,</u> <u>be sober,</u> and <u>hope to the end for the grace that is to be brought unto you at the revelation of Jesus Christ;</u>

Remember, the word "grace" means "gift." Let us put this into a "to do" list: (1) be unchanging in the knowledge of your salvation, (2) be of sound mind, and (3) hold onto the hope which has been revealed to you concerning the good news of the Kingdom.

God has had plans for Israel since their very beginning. He is molding Israel into becoming a holy nation, a royal priesthood. In the coming Kingdom, they will stand between their God and the nations. True Israel must not be lured away by worldly things as they have been in the past. Then, they did it in ignorance. Verse 14:

14 As obedient children, not fashioning yourselves according to the former lusts in your ignorance:

Life for them is different now. They are beginning to see more clearly their destiny. Peter is going to disclose something to them: their "raison d'être" or their "reason for being."

Nearly fourteen hundred years before Peter wrote this letter, Moses recorded these words from God. Exodus 19:5-6:

> 5 **Now therefore, if ye [Israel] will obey my voice indeed, and keep my covenant, then <u>ye shall be a peculiar treasure unto me</u> above all people: for all the earth is mine:**
>
> 6 **<u>And ye shall be unto me a kingdom of priests, and an holy nation</u>. These are the words which thou shalt speak unto the children of Israel.**

God created the nation of Israel for Himself. The word "peculiar" means "belonging to a person and only that person." He created this "peculiar" nation for a very special purpose. That purpose will be fulfilled when David's Kingdom is established again by God's eternal King. God's Word guaranties it!

In the following, the word "holy" does not mean perfect. It means "separated." God does not require that a man can be perfect. However, He does expect His people to be "separated from the world." 1 Peter 1:15-16:

> 15 **But as he which hath called you is**

holy, so be ye holy in all manner of conversation; 16 Because it is written, Be ye holy; for I am holy.

God has separated Himself from what is worldly and He expects Israel to do the same. The word "conversation" means "manner of living." They must not live in the same manner as the other nations who are heathen.

All men are to be judged according to their works. Those works which are contrary to God's Law are punishable by death. They stand already condemned to death because of their actions. The word "redeem" means "to buy back" something. There was only one way that sinners can be "redeemed" or bought back from death. Verses 17-19:

17 And if ye call on the Father, who without respect of persons judgeth according to every man's work, pass the time of your sojourning here in fear:

18 Forasmuch as ye know that <u>ye were not redeemed with corruptible things</u>, as silver and gold, from your vain conversation received by tradition from your fathers;

19 <u>But with the precious blood of Christ,</u> as of a lamb without blemish and without spot:

Notice that observing the customs and traditions of their fathers are vain or useless. It is the precious blood of Jesus Christ, their Messiah, that paid the price of their redemption.

Peter continues with describing their Savior in verses 20-21:

20 Who verily was foreordained before the foundation of the world, but was manifest [made known] in these last times for you,

21 Who by him do believe in God, that raised him up from the dead, and gave him glory; <u>that your faith and hope might be in God.</u>

God knew before the Creation what would need to be done. Now, God's work has been made known to the Jews. For what purpose? So that their "faith and hope might be in God."

As we come to the end of this chapter, we must remember that Peter is writing to the faithful and true Israel. They heard the Good News of the Kingdom and believed. Now, he encourages them to live according to their faith. Verses 22-23:

> **22 Seeing ye have purified your souls in obeying the truth through the Spirit unto unfeigned love of the brethren, see that ye love one another with a pure heart fervently:**

> **23 <u>Being born again, not of corruptible seed, but of incorruptible, by the word of God, which liveth and abideth forever.</u>**

Peter concludes with the frailty of Mankind, but knowing the Word of God endures forever. Verses 24-25:

> **24 For all flesh is as grass, and all the glory of man as the flower of grass. The grass withereth, and the flower thereof falleth away:**

> **25 But the word of the Lord endureth forever. And this is the word which by the gospel is preached unto you.**

9

1 Peter 2

The Kingdom Believers have heard the gospel of their salvation preached to them. God has provided them with an understanding of His desire for their manner of living and their future. Now, they must continue to grow in His Word. 1 Peter 2:1-3:

> 1 **Wherefore laying aside all malice, and all guile, and hypocrisies, and envies, and all evil speakings,**
>
> 2 **As newborn babes, desire the sincere milk of the word, that ye may grow thereby:** 3 **If so be ye have tasted that the Lord is gracious.**

Peter teaches that Jesus Christ as a "living stone" and, like Him, the believers will be "living stones" as well. How is that possible? Christ is their Priest and, like Him, they are to become a holy priesthood. Verses 4-5:

> 4 **To whom coming, as unto a living stone, disallowed indeed of men, but chosen of God, and precious,**
>
> 5 **Ye also, as lively stones, are built up a spiritual house, an <u>holy priesthood</u>, to offer up spiritual sacrifices, acceptable to God by Jesus Christ.**

In the Old Testament, God used prophets to carry His Words to the people. He also used priests to represent the people in their relationship with God. But, to whom are these Kingdom Believers to be priests?

Peter quotes the Prophet Isaiah. (See Isa. 28:16.) He assures these believers that they will not be "confounded" or "confused." Verse 6:

> 6 **Wherefore also it is contained in the scripture, Behold, I lay in Sion a chief corner stone, elect, precious: and he that believeth on him shall not be confounded.**

He compares the value of the "living stone" to the

believers and the value to those who do not believe. Verse 7:

> 7 **Unto you therefore which believe he is precious: but unto them which be disobedient, the stone which the builders disallowed, the same is made the head of the corner,**

The disobedient "stumbled" over its message and they rejected Him as their Messiah. Verse 8:

> 8 **And a stone of stumbling, and a rock of offence, even to them which stumble at the word, being disobedient: whereunto also they were appointed.**

God knew this would happen and, therefore, Peter could say that to this end "they were appointed." This testing or trying of Israel is like the "refiner's fire." Its purpose is to remove impurities until all that is left is pure. Malachi, the last book in the Old Testament, recorded this. Malachi 3:3:

> 3 **And he [God] shall sit as a refiner and purifier of silver: and he shall purify the sons of Levi, and purge them as gold and silver, that they may offer unto the LORD an offering in righteousness.**

Israel is undergoing a purification to become priests so that "they may offer unto the LORD an offering in righteousness."

As Peter continues he hit the summation of who true and faithful Israel is. 1 Peter 2:9-10:

> 9 **But ye are a chosen generation, <u>a royal priesthood</u>, <u>an holy nation</u>, <u>a peculiar people</u>; that ye should shew forth the praises of him who hath called you out of darkness into his marvellous light:**
>
> 10 **Which in time past were not a people, but are <u>now the people of God</u>: which had not obtained mercy, but <u>now have obtained mercy</u>.**

He earnestly implores them to live a life worthy of their calling. Their "conversation" or their "manner of living" among the Gentiles must be honest so that they will glorify God. Verses 11-12:

> 11 **Dearly beloved, I beseech you as strangers and pilgrims, abstain from fleshly lusts, which war against the soul;**
>
> 12 **Having your conversation honest**

**among the Gentiles: that, whereas they
speak against you as evildoers, they
may by your good works, which they
shall behold, glorify God in the day of
visitation.**

We already asked the question: "for whom are these
believers to be priests?" Let us better answer that
with a breakdown of humanity in general.

At the Tower of Babel, God scattered the people and this was the beginning of "the nations." Each
nation had their distinctive tongue or language. Out
of all the nations, God called one man named Abraham to become an "holy nation" for Himself. They
would later become a nation of priests who would
intercede on behalf of the other nations – the Gentiles. God created a third group through the Apostle
Paul who refers to new group as neither Jew nor
Gentile. (See Gal. 3:28; Col. 3:11.) This new group re-
ceives its salvation from God by grace through faith
alone. Their removal happens at what is called the
"Rapture." This will occur prior to the beginning of
the seven years of Jacob's testing.3 It will be the Gentiles who will seek out the Jews to act as a liaison,

---

3 The books *Letters to Theophilus* and *The Glorious Destiny of Israel* provide systematic explanations of their differ-
ences in God's plan for the restoration of His Creation.

their representative, or their priest to interact with God their Creator on their behalf.

The Prophet Zechariah tells of these future days. Zechariah 8:22-23:

> **22 Yea, many people and strong nations shall come to seek the LORD of hosts in Jerusalem, and to pray before the LORD.**
>
> **23 Thus saith the LORD of hosts; In those days it shall come to pass, that ten men shall take hold out of all languages of the nations, even shall take hold of the skirt of him that is a Jew, saying, We will go with you: for we have heard that God is with you.**

You can see Israel's importance to God's plan. They will be God's royal priesthood. We just read that the Gentiles should see their good works and "glorify God in the day of visitation." This "day of visitation" is the day the Lord Jesus Christ returns. Gentiles who remained favorable to the Jews during the Tribulation will continue on earth. Therefore, true Israel, as a priesthood, will intercede of behalf of these nations or Gentiles.

Having this promise of the mantel of priesthood upon them, their lives must be exemplary or above reproach. Peter gives them instructions as to how they should act in verses 13-17:

> 13 **Submit yourselves to every ordinance of man for the Lord's sake: whether it be to the king, as supreme; 14 Or unto governors, as unto them that are sent by him for the punishment of evildoers, and for the praise of them that do well.**
>
> 15 **For so is the will of God, that with well doing ye may put to silence the ignorance of foolish men: 16 As free, and not using your liberty for a cloke of maliciousness, but as the servants of God.**
>
> 17 **Honour all men. Love the brotherhood. Fear God. Honour the king.**

If they do this, then they will be above reproach among all the people.

He now gives instructions to servants who are subject to their earthly masters. Similarly, employees are subject to their bosses. The word "froward" (correct spelling) has a deep meaning. It means "turning away from with an aversion or distain; a lack of willingness to yield or comply with what is required; being unmanageable or disobedient." This would certainly not make for an ideal employee! Verses 18-20:

> 18 Servants, be subject to your masters with all fear; not only to the good and gentle, but also to the froward. 19 For this is thankworthy, if a man for conscience toward God endure grief, suffering wrongfully.
>
> 20 For what glory is it, if, when ye be buffeted for your faults, ye shall take it patiently? but if, when ye do well, and suffer for it, ye take it patiently, this is acceptable with God.

They are called to "endure unto the end" through trials and tribulations because they know the hope that God has set aside for them.

The word "even" often means "that is to say" or "in other words" and it repeats or emphasizes something previous said. Let us try this in verses 21-24:

> 21 For even [that is to say] hereunto were ye called: because Christ also suffered

for us, leaving us an example, that ye should follow his steps:

22 Who did no sin, neither was guile found in his mouth: 23 Who, when he was reviled, reviled not again; when he suffered, he threatened not; but committed himself to him that [God Who] judgeth righteously:

24 Who [upon] his own self bare [bore] our sins in his own body on the tree, that we, being dead to sins, should live unto righteousness: by whose stripes ye were healed.

Christ was insulted, rebuked, mocked, spat upon, and mistreated. Yet He remained committed to His calling from God. While He bore His shame, He did not waver in His conviction.

True or faithful Israel are to be like Him Who saved them. Christ is to be their example. Consider Isaiah's words in view of this. Isaiah 53:6-7:

6 All we like sheep have gone astray; we have turned every one to his own way; and the LORD hath laid on him the iniquity of us all.

7 He was oppressed, and he was afflicted, yet he opened not his mouth: he is brought as a lamb to the slaughter, and as a sheep before her shearers is dumb, so he openeth not his mouth.

Notice that Christ took His sufferings when He could have called ten thousand angels to destroy the world and set Him free. Yet, He did not.

Jesus Christ said that He was the Shepherd to His sheep. John 10:11:

11 I am the good shepherd: the good shepherd giveth his life for the sheep.

King David wrote, "The Lord is my Shepherd, I shall not want . . ." (Ps. 23:1). As their Shepherd Who cares for His sheep, He laid down His life for them. The book of Hebrews tells us that He is now High Priest of the order of Melchizedek. He is also their Bishop or Overseer. True and faithful Israel now knows the truth. God has given them hopes and promises. Jesus Christ, their High Priest, will watch over His sheep. Jesus said, "My sheep hear my voice, and I know them, and they follow me" (Jn. 10:27). Verse 25:

25 For ye were as sheep going astray; but are now returned unto the Shepherd

and Bishop of your souls.

10

1 Peter 3

The home is the center of Jewish life. God created the family unit as the building block for the people of His creation. The Jews practiced a patriarchal authority where the husband was the head of the household. Today, from what I have personally observed, this is less likely the case in modern Jewish households. Peter gives instruction to the Kingdom Believers concerning wives. 1 Peter 3:1:

> 1 **Likewise, ye wives, be in subjection to your own husbands; that, if any obey not the word, they also may without the word be won by the conversation of the wives;**

Should any husband not obey the Word acting contrary to God's instructions, these husbands may be won over by their wife's "conversation" or "manner of living." So, that by the wife's example, the husband may see their "chaste" or "pure" manner of living and gain respect for God. Verse 2:

> 2 **While they behold your chaste conversation coupled with fear.**

He continues by addressing how wives should adorn themselves. God does not look at the outside, but considers the heart. Verses 3-4:

> 3 **Whose adorning let it not be that outward adorning of plaiting the hair, and of wearing of gold, or of putting on of apparel;**

> 4 **But let it be the hidden man of the heart, in that which is not corruptible, even the ornament of a meek and quiet spirit, which is in the sight of God of great price.**

God holds a "meek and quiet spirit" of a wife to be of great value. Peter looks back at Sarah, Abraham's wife. He uses Sarah as an example of a wife that other wives should emulate. Verses 5-6:

> 5 **For after this manner in the old time**

the holy women also, who trusted in God, adorned themselves, being in subjection unto their own husbands:

6 Even [that is to say] as Sara obeyed Abraham, calling him lord: whose daughters ye are, as long as ye do well, and are not afraid with any amazement.

Here, I believe the word "amazement" means "disbelief" or "lack of trust" in God. Knowing the truth, wives need not fear but be like Sarah, "who trusted in God."

Peter turns his attention to the husbands. They are to esteem and honor their wives. These are similar to the instructions given by Paul to those saved by the Gospel of Grace. However, these Jewish Believers are warned of a consequence. God sees the husband and wife as being co-heirs to salvation. If the husband fails to observe Peter's instruction, then answers to his prayers may be "hindered." Verse 7:

7 Likewise, ye husbands, dwell with them according to knowledge, giving honour unto the wife, as unto the weaker vessel, and as being heirs together of the grace of life; that your prayers be not hindered.

He now addresses all believers. They should be of one mind – in agreement. Note the word "pitiful" means "full of tenderness and compassion." Verse 8:

8 Finally, be ye all of one mind, having compassion one of another, love as brethren, be pitiful, be courteous:

They must not retaliate – repaying evil with evil. As priests, they will be called to bless those who curse them. Look at the words of Christ in Matthew 5:43-45:

43 Ye have heard that it hath been said, Thou shalt love thy neighbour, and hate thine enemy.

44 But I say unto you, <u>Love your enemies, bless them that curse you, do good to them that hate you, and pray for them which despitefully use you, and persecute you;</u>

45 <u>That ye may be the children of your Father</u> which is in heaven: for he maketh his sun to rise on the evil and on the good, and sendeth rain on the just and on the unjust.

Compare the above verses to what Peter writes to them in 1 Peter 3:9-10:

9 Not rendering evil for evil, or railing for railing: but contrariwise blessing; knowing that ye are thereunto called, that ye should inherit a blessing.

10 For he that will love life, and see good days, let him refrain his tongue from evil, and his lips that they speak no guile:

The word "eschew" means "to flee from; to shun or avoid." This is the opposite of the word "ensue" which means "to seek after or to follow." Verse 11:

11 Let him eschew evil, and do good; let him seek peace, and ensue it.

Peter tells them to shun evil and seek after peace in verse 12:

12 For the eyes of the Lord are over the righteous, and his ears are open unto their prayers: but the face of the Lord is against them that do evil.

There is a benefit for following these instructions.

Verses 13-14:

> 13 And who is he that will harm you, if ye be followers of that which is good? 14 But and if ye suffer for righteousness' sake, happy are ye: and be not afraid of their terror, neither be troubled;

The verb "sanctify" means "to separate" or "set apart." It has to do with clinging onto what is of God and shunning what is of the world. Verses 15-17:

> 15 But sanctify the Lord God in your hearts: and be ready always to give an answer to every man that asketh you a reason of the hope that is in you with meekness and fear:

> 16 Having a good conscience; that, whereas they speak evil of you, as of evildoers, they may be ashamed that falsely accuse your good conversation in Christ.

> 17 For it is better, if the will of God be so, that ye suffer for well doing, than for evil doing.

Suffering that comes from doing what is good is not

from God. Look at Christ. He suffered also while doing God's work on earth. God blessed Him by raising Him from the dead. Verse 18:

18 For Christ also hath once suffered for sins, the just for the unjust, that he might bring us to God, being put to death in the flesh, but quickened [made alive] by the Spirit:

There is a common belief, based upon a version of the Apostles' Creed. It states that Jesus Christ "was crucified, dead, and buried" and continues by declaring that "He descended into hell…" The Jews would understand this since they are familiar with Sheol. Hades or Sheol is a temporary holding place. Many people confuse this with Hell which is the destination for eternal judgment. Jesus did not go to a place of judgment or punishment following His death. He descended into Hades or Sheol. We can see from this story Jesus told. Luke 16:19-26:

19 There was a certain rich man, which was clothed in purple and fine linen, and fared sumptuously every day:

20 And there was a certain beggar named Lazarus, which was laid at his gate, full of sores, 21 And desiring to be fed with

the crumbs which fell from the rich man's table: moreover the dogs came and licked his sores.

22 And it came to pass, that the beggar died, and was carried by the angels into Abraham's bosom: the rich man also died, and was buried;

23 And in hell [Sheol] he lift up his eyes, being in torments, and seeth Abraham afar off, and Lazarus in his bosom.

24 And he cried and said, Father Abraham, have mercy on me, and send Lazarus, that he may dip the tip of his finger in water, and cool my tongue; for I am tormented in this flame.

25 But Abraham said, Son, remember that thou in thy lifetime receivedst thy good things, and likewise Lazarus evil things: but now he is comforted, and thou art tormented.

26 And beside all this, between us and you there is a great gulf fixed: so that they which would pass from hence to you cannot; neither can they pass to us,

that would come from thence.

There is a clear division with a great gulf fixed between them. One side is where the righteous wait and the other side where unrighteous wait for the resurrection. Yes, all will be resurrected according to Jesus Who is appointed as Judge. These words from Jesus will tie it all together for us. John 5:26-29:

> 26 **For as the Father hath life in himself; so hath he given to the Son to have life in himself; 27 And hath given him authority to execute judgment also, because he is the Son of man.**

> 28 **Marvel not at this: for the hour is coming, in the which all that are in the graves shall hear his voice,**

> 29 **And shall come forth; they that have done good, unto the resurrection of life; and they that have done evil, unto the resurrection of damnation.**

Peter referred to Jesus' visit to Sheol. Since they are held there until the judgement, he calls it a "prison." Verses 19-20:

> 19 **By which also he [Christ] went and**

preached unto the spirits in prison;

20 Which sometime were disobedient, when once the longsuffering of God waited in the days of Noah, while the ark was a preparing [being prepared], wherein few, that is, eight souls were saved by water.

During Noah's time, the Flood was a judgment upon the earth. It killed millions of people by it spared eight people of faith: Noah, his three sons, and their wives.

This Great Flood was a "type" or example of something else yet to come. It was a "type" or representation of baptism or washing. Verse 21:

21 The like figure whereunto even baptism doth also now save us (not the putting away of the filth of the flesh, but the answer of a good conscience toward God,) by the resurrection of Jesus Christ:

In the Kingdom Gospel, baptism becomes an important part of the Jews' process of salvation. The components are repentance and baptism. The word "repentance" means "putting away the filth of the flesh and maintaining a good conscience before God." This is followed by baptism which represents the death and resurrection of their Messiah. Afterwards, the Jews must continue in living faith exhibiting good works. All this, they must do and while enduring unto Messiah's return.

After Christ descended into Hades, He ascended into heaven. Look at what King David wrote in Psalms 110:1:

> 1 **The LORD said unto my Lord, Sit thou at my right hand, until I make thine enemies thy footstool.**

Let us compare this to what Peter wrote at the conclusion of this chapter. 1 Peter 3:22:

> 22 **Who [Christ] is gone into heaven, and is on the right hand of God; angels and authorities and powers being made subject unto him.**

11

1 Peter 4

Peter points to Christ's suffering and to the fact that He suffered in the flesh for them. 1 Peter 4:1:

1 Forasmuch then as Christ hath suffered for us in the flesh, arm yourselves likewise with the same mind: for he that hath suffered in the flesh hath ceased from sin;

In the same manner as Christ, Who was sinless, they are to arm or guard themselves with like mindedness. Christ died to the flesh and when resurrected receiving a glorified body.

Now glorified, Christ no longer lives among sinful men who lived according to the flesh. Instead, He sits at the right hand of God Almighty and serves

Him in glory. Verse 2:

> **2 That he no longer should live the rest of his time in the flesh to the lusts of men, but to the will of God.**

Peter compares believers to Christ. In the following, Gentiles represent godlessness and are sometimes called "heathen." Verses 3-4:

> **3 For the time past of our life may suffice us to have wrought [worked] the will of the Gentiles, when we walked in lasciviousness, lusts, excess of wine, revellings, banquetings, and abominable idolatries:**

> **4 Wherein they think it strange that ye run not with them to the same excess of riot, [therefore] speaking evil of you:**

The Gentiles look at the Jews and think it strange that, for some reason, the Jews do not do what they do. It is because of this that they judge and speak badly about them.

He asks about those who will be judged. For only Christ is able to judge the living and the dead. Verse 5:

100

5 Who shall give account to him that is ready to judge the quick [living] and the dead.

It was for this reason that Christ descended into Hades to preach the gospel to those Jews who were dead.

6 For this cause [reason] was the gospel preached also to them that are dead, that they might be judged according to men in the flesh, but live according to God in the spirit.

The judgement of men according to sin is death, but life is given to those who are saved according to the Spirit.

I am going to take a break from the text and tell you a short story. As often as I can, I share the Gospel of Grace with people: friends, relatives, neighbors. One person objected to God's judging people who have never heard the gospel. He thought it was unfair. Furthermore, he was not interested in a God Who was unfair. This was a teaching opportunity. It gave me a lesson to learn for a better response to this objection in the future. I am actually grateful to this neighbor for this lesson.

We are going to take a look at what Jesus taught the Jews about judging each other. It will make sense and, more importantly, it will tie into the last verse we already read: 1 Peter 5:6. Here is what Jesus said in Matthew 7:1-2:

> 1 **Judge not, that ye be not judged.** 2 <u>**For with what judgment ye judge, ye shall be judged**</u>: and <u>**with what measure ye mete, it shall be measured to you**</u> again.

What if, when men judge others, they are actually establishing a precedent which becomes the basis for condemning themselves? That is why Christ was cautioning the Jews not to judge others? That is my explanation of the words, "that they might be judged according to men in the flesh." How can someone refute a judgment they proclaimed as just on someone else?

The end of this current Age of Grace is imminent. Once this happens, the Mosaic Age which was in suspension will resume. There are only seven years before the end times Jesus described in Matthew 24.[4] 1 Peter 4:7:

---

[4] For a detailed explanation of the seven ages and how they relate to Israel, refer to *The Glorious Destiny of Israel*

7 But <u>the end of all things is at hand</u>: be ye therefore sober, and watch unto prayer.

In view of the Tribulation, now imminent, Peter gives additional instruction. Verses 8-10:

8 And above all things have fervent charity among yourselves: for charity shall cover the multitude of sins.

9 Use hospitality one to another without grudging. 10 As every man hath received the gift, even so minister the same one to another, as good stewards of the manifold grace of God.

Kingdom Believers are to be good stewards and use their "manifold grace" or their "many diverse gifts" to minister to one another.

Some men have the ability to speak, Peter cautions them. If they do speak, then they should speak according to their ability and it should not be empty or vain words. It should be concerning what God has spoken. Verse 11:

–*The Fulfillment of the Promises and Prophecies To Israel* published by GraceWord Publishing.

11 If any man speak, let him speak as [concerning] the oracles of God; if any man minister, let him do it as of the ability which God giveth: that God in all things may be glorified through Jesus Christ, to whom be praise and dominion for ever and ever. Amen.

By doing this, in all things it may glorify God by His Son Jesus Christ.

The believers are concerning about what is coming. Matthew 24 paints a dismal picture of what will transpire in these last seven years. Peter offers them encouragement with consolation concerning the Tribulation. Verses 12-14:

12 Beloved, think it not strange concerning the fiery trial which is to try you, as though some strange thing happened unto you: **13** But rejoice, inasmuch as ye are partakers of Christ's sufferings; that, when his glory shall be revealed, ye may be glad also with exceeding joy.

14 If ye be reproached for the name of Christ, happy are ye; for the spirit of glory and of God resteth upon you: on their part he is evil spoken of, but on

your part he is glorified.

He cautions them that they will not escape judgment. Verse 15:

> 15 **But let none of you suffer as a murderer, or as a thief, or as an evildoer, or as a busybody in other men's matters.**

The word "Christian" means "a follower of Christ" and faithful Israel is following Christ. If any believer suffer, then they should not feel humiliated. Instead, let them glorify God that they were worthy to suffer as Christ did. Verse 16:

> 16 **Yet if any man suffer as a Christian, let him not be ashamed; but let him glorify God on this behalf.**

Peter wrote this letter almost two thousand years ago. At the time, they believed the judgment was imminent. As of this writing, it is still eminent. There is only one thing holding it back. What is that?

In his letter to the Grace Believers in Rome, Paul devoted a good portion of it to explaining what was presently going on with Israel. (See Romans 6-9.) This is the condensed answer to that question. Romans 11:25-27:

25 For I would not, brethren, that ye should be ignorant of this mystery, lest ye should be wise in your own conceits; that blindness in part is happened to Israel, <u>until the fulness of the Gentiles be come in.</u>

26 And so all Israel shall be saved: as it is written, <u>There shall come out of Sion the Deliverer, and shall turn away ungodliness from Jacob:</u>

27 <u>For this is my covenant unto them, when I shall take away their sins.</u>

God has predetermined what the "fulness of the Gentiles" will be. Once that had happened, those saved by the Gospel of Grace will be removed. This leaves Israel and the nations to battle it out until their King returns.

If judgment must start, then it must start with the believers. Israel will be tested. They do have a High Priest in heaven Who oversees them. Until He returns as their King, they must keep the faith and be righteous like Him. Verses 17-18:

17 For the time is come that <u>judgment must begin at the house of God</u>: and if it first begin at us, what shall the end be of them that obey not the gospel of God?

18 And if the righteous scarcely be saved, where shall the ungodly and the sinner appear?

The faithful of Israel have a hope. Their hope is in their God. Psalms 33:18-22:

18 Behold, the eye of the LORD is upon them that fear him, upon them that hope in his mercy;

19 To deliver their soul from death, and to keep them alive in famine.

20 Our soul waiteth for the LORD: he is our help and our shield.

21 For our heart shall rejoice in him, because we have trusted in his holy name.

22 <u>Let thy mercy, O LORD, be upon us, according as we hope in thee</u>.

There is hope for the faithful who "commit the keeping of their souls to Him." Verse 19:

19 Wherefore let them that suffer according to the will of God <u>commit the keeping of their souls to him</u> in well doing, as unto a faithful Creator.

12

1 Peter 5

Peter writes to the elders of an assembly. The word "exhort" means "to encourage, to embolden, to cheer on or to advise." 1 Peter 5:1:

> 1 **The elders which are among you I exhort, who am also an elder, and a witness of the sufferings of Christ, and also a partaker of the glory that shall be revealed:**

Not only is Peter an elder, but he witnessed the suffering of the Christ. He was with the Messiah from His early ministry to His ascension. And, like them, he too is a partaker in the hope of the glory to come.

As an apostle, he gives them instructions for the care of the believers. Verses 2-4:

2 Feed the flock of God which is among you, taking the oversight thereof, not by constraint, but willingly; not for filthy lucre, but of a ready mind;

3 Neither as being lords over God's heritage, but being ensamples [examples] to the flock.

4 And when the chief Shepherd shall appear, ye shall receive a crown of glory that fadeth not away.

If the caretakers of the sheep are diligent in their care, then they will receive a reward from the Shepherd Himself – a crown of glory that will not fade away.

He writes to the younger among the believers giving them sound advice. Verses 5-7:

5 Likewise, ye younger, submit yourselves unto the elder. Yea, all of you be subject one to another, and be clothed with humility: for God resisteth the proud, and giveth grace to the humble.

6 Humble yourselves therefore under the mighty hand of God, that he may exalt you in due time:

7 Casting all your care upon him; for he careth for you.

Since the younger are more likely to be attacked by predators, he cautions them about the cunning of the adversary. Verses 8-9:

8 Be sober, be vigilant; because your adversary the devil, as a roaring lion, walketh about, seeking whom he may devour:

9 Whom resist stedfast in the faith, knowing that the same afflictions are accomplished in your brethren that are in the world.

Although the verses immediately following seem to be directed to those younger believers, they serve to benefit all the believers. Remember, these epistles were read aloud to the entire assembly. Verses 10-11:

10 But the God of all grace, who hath called us unto his eternal glory by Christ Jesus, after that ye have suffered a while, make you perfect, stablish, strengthen, settle you.

11 To him be glory and dominion for

ever and ever. Amen.

As with most of the epistles, personal notes are included at the end because of relationships among the brethren. It appears that Silvanus was Peter's amanuensis. This is a "scribe who writes as the author dictates" the letter. They are often used because of their superior penmanship or a disability of the author. The name Silvanus is a derivation of Silas. This may be the same Silas who accompanied Paul on his missionary journeys. Verse 12:

12 **By Silvanus, a faithful brother unto you, as I suppose, I have written briefly, exhorting, and testifying that this is the true grace of God wherein ye stand.**

The last verses provide some intrigue. The City of Babylon had been reduced to a desert outpost before Peter's time and was eventually abandoned. There is no record of any assembly located there. Peter may have made a figurative comparison with the evil city of Rome. It was there that Peter would be executed. Verse 13:

13 **The church that is at Babylon, elected together with you, saluteth you; and so doth Marcus my son.**

It is believed that Marcus is Mark who he refers to as his "son" in the faith.

With these final notes, Peter concludes his letter with a blessing to his fellow believers who are all in Christ Jesus. Verse 14:

14 **Greet ye one another with a kiss of charity. Peace be with you all that are in Christ Jesus. Amen.**

13

2 Peter 1

Peter's second epistle was intended for a larger group of people. These original epistles would be copied in the same manner the Jews had done for centuries. These copies would be shared with other assemblies. In Paul's letter to the Romans, he asked this question. "What advantage then hath the Jew? or what profit is there of circumcision?" Then, he gave this answer, "Much every way: chiefly, because that unto them were committed the oracles of God" (Rom. 3:1-2). The Jews were entrusted with God's Word. All believers owe their gratitude to them.

He begins with this salutation. 2 Peter 1:1:

1 Simon Peter, a servant and an apostle of Jesus Christ, to them that have ob- tained like precious faith with us

**through the righteousness of God and
our Saviour Jesus Christ:**

He writes to this broad group of Kingdom Believers
who have the same faith. Their faith and hope are in
the righteousness of God and His Son.

God has provided them with "the knowledge
of him." This is something that unbelievers cannot
say. God has made promises to Israel and, because
they believe, those promises are theirs. Verses 2-4:

> **2 Grace and peace be multiplied unto
> you through the knowledge of God, and
> of Jesus our Lord, 3 According as his di-
> vine power hath given unto us all
> things that pertain unto life and godli-
> ness, through the knowledge of him
> that hath called us to glory and virtue:**

> **4 Whereby are given unto us exceeding
> great and precious promises: that by
> these ye might be partakers of the di-
> vine nature, having escaped the corrup-
> tion that is in the world through lust.**

Their faith is the foundation of their relationship with God. Peter calls them to build upon that
faith. Next, they should add virtue and to that they

should add knowledge by continually studying His Word. Verse 5:

> 5 **And beside this, giving all diligence, add to your faith virtue; and to virtue knowledge;**

There is more. Peter continues to strengthen the believers. Like building blocks, he begins with the foundation which is faith. Verses 6-7:

> 6 **And to knowledge temperance; and to temperance patience; and to patience godliness; 7 And to godliness brotherly kindness; and to brotherly kindness charity.**

It is easy to read through this quickly and move on. But, Kingdom Believers should stop and look at the progression that Peter chose. Notice faith is the basis of everything else. For without faith, no one is a believer. Each believer must have faith and trust the Word of God individually. Here it is again.

FAITH + VIRTUE + KNOWLEDGE + TEMPERENCE + PATIENCE + GODLINESS + BROTHERLY KINDNESS + CHARITY

For those who follow the Kingdom Gospel, this is a great reminder to put on the front of their refrigerator! Peter put a lot of thought into creating this list. Each item being a building block set upon another.

In the gospels, Jesus often told parables about producing fruit. He once cursed a fig tree because it did not yield the fruit that was expected. We can find that story in Matthew 21:18-22 and Mark 11:12-14. The fig tree was representative of the nation of Israel. God had planted them in the Promised Land and they had failed to produce fruit. Verses 8-9:

> **8 For if these things be in you, and abound, they make you that ye shall neither be barren nor unfruitful in the knowledge of our Lord Jesus Christ.**
>
> **9 But he that lacketh these things is blind, and cannot see afar off, and hath forgotten that he was purged from his old sins.**

This is his point. Believers are to bear fruit. Why? Like a tree, it must bear fruit as evidence of life. The quality of its fruit confirms the value of the fruit tree to its owner.

Throughout Israel history, their faith failed repeatedly. Therefore, they must give heed to God's requirement for good works. Why? It confirms their salvation and assures their entrance into "the everlasting kingdom of our Lord and Saviour Jesus Christ." Verses 10-11:

> 10 **Wherefore the rather, brethren, give diligence to <u>make your calling and election sure</u>: for if ye do these things, ye shall never fall:**

> 11 **For so an entrance shall be ministered unto you abundantly into the everlasting kingdom of our Lord and Saviour Jesus Christ.**

Peter is compelled to remind them of these important facts. Their salvation depends upon it. Verse 12:

> 12 **Wherefore I will not be negligent to put you always in remembrance of these things, though ye know them, and be established in the present truth.**

The word "meet" means "proper, suitable, or fit for its purpose." Verses 13-14:

> 13 **Yea, I think it meet, as long as I am in**

this tabernacle, to stir you up by putting you in remembrance;

14 Knowing that shortly I must put off this my tabernacle, even as our Lord Jesus Christ hath shewed me.

The Lord has made Peter aware that his time is short, therefore he wastes no time urging them. Verse 15:

15 Moreover I will endeavour that ye may be able after my decease to have these things always in remembrance.

Peter has become aware that his death is imminent. Therefore, he puts these things into writing so that believers can remember them. These points are as important today for Kingdom Believers as they were when Peter wrote them.

He speaks collectively about himself and the other apostles who preached the Gospel of the Kingdom. They are not making this up. In fact, they were all eyewitnesses of the earthly ministry of the Son of God. Verse 16:

16 <u>For we have not followed cunningly devised fables</u>, when we made known unto you the power and coming of our

Lord Jesus Christ, <u>but were eyewit-</u>
<u>nesses of his majesty.</u>

They heard and saw and fellowshipped with Him.
God proclaims Jesus as His Son twice. The first was
at His baptism by John the Baptist. The second was
at the Transfiguration.

In this record of the Transfiguration, pay atten-
tion to the mention of the Gospel of the Kingdom.
Notice who was with Jesus at that time. It empowers
Peter's testimony even more. Mark 9:1-8:

> 1 **And he said unto them, Verily I say**
> **unto you, That there be some of them**
> **that stand here, which shall not taste of**
> **death, till they have seen the kingdom**
> **of God come with power.**
>
> 2 **And after six days Jesus taketh with**
> **him Peter, and James, and John, and**
> **leadeth them up into an high mountain**
> **apart by themselves: and he was trans-**
> **figured before them.** 3 **And his raiment**
> **became shining, exceeding white as**
> **snow; so as no fuller on earth can white**
> **them.**
>
> 4 **And there appeared unto them Elias**

with Moses: and they were talking with Jesus. 5 And Peter answered and said to Jesus, Master, it is good for us to be here: and let us make three tabernacles; one for thee, and one for Moses, and one for Elias. 6 For he wist [knew] not what to say; for they were sore afraid.

7 And there was a cloud that overshadowed them: and a voice came out of the cloud, saying, <u>This is my beloved Son: hear him</u>. 8 And suddenly, when they had looked round about, they saw no man anymore, save Jesus only with themselves.

With this information, let us continue with our text. 2 Peter 1:17-18:

17 For he received from God the Father honour and glory, when there came such a voice to him from the excellent glory, This is my beloved Son, in whom I am well pleased.

18 And this voice which came from heaven we heard, when we were with him in the holy mount.

They gave their eyewitness testimony of God's Son having witnessed all that happened. To this, add the testimony of the prophets. 2 Peter 1:19:

19 We have also a more sure word of prophecy; whereunto ye do well that ye take heed, as unto a light that shineth in a dark place, until the day dawn, and the day star arise in your hearts:

The day that will dawn will be the Day of the Lord's Coming. There are very few stars observed with the naked eye during the day. However, this Day Star will be seen by everyone!

Prophecy is God speaking about the future. It can be identified by the use of the future tense of the verbs. In other words, God is saying what He "will" do. A prophet does not speak his own words or opinions. He gives the words that he received from God. Therefore, prophecy must not be interpreted subjectively, but objectively. All biblical prophecy is given by revelation. All biblical prophecy was intended for Israel. If there are any Grace Believers who are reading this book, then you must know this. There is no prophecy for anyone other than Israel. Therefore, when interpreting prophecy, it must always be viewed in light of Israel and their future. Verses 20-21:

20 Knowing this first, that no prophecy of the scripture is of any private interpretation.

21 For the prophecy came not in old time by the will of man: but holy men of God spake as they were moved by the Holy Ghost.

14

2 Peter 2

In the previous chapter, Peter wrote about the purpose of the prophets. Now, he compares God's prophets with false prophets. We must remember that the writers of these Hebrew epistles continued the teaching of Christ's earthly ministry. Nothing changed. The Messiah came for the lost sheep of the house of Israel (*cf.* Matt. 10:6; 15:24). He came to fulfill the promises made to the fathers (*cf.* Rom. 15:8). At the Ascension, He commanded them concerning His sheep, "Teaching them to observe all things whatsoever I have commanded you . . ." (Matt. 28:20). They "observe" by "doing."

Let us look at Jesus' words when He answered the disciples' question, "Tell us, when shall these things be? and what shall be the sign of thy coming, and of the end of the world?" (Matt. 24:3). Peter was there and heard Him answer. Notice what He said about the false prophets during the end times:

Matthew 24:11:

> 11 And <u>many false prophets</u> shall rise, and shall deceive many.

Matthew 24:23-26:

> 23 Then if any man shall say unto you, Lo, here is Christ, or there; believe it not. 24 For <u>there shall arise false Christs, and false prophets</u>, and shall shew great signs and wonders; insomuch that, if it were possible, they shall deceive the very elect.
>
> 25 Behold, I have told you before. 26 Wherefore if they shall say unto you, Behold, he is in the desert; go not forth: behold, he is in the secret chambers; <u>believe it not</u>.

Peter begins this letter by warning believers not to fall prey to these deceivers. 2 Peter 2:1-2:

> 1 But there were false prophets also

among the people, even as there shall be false teachers among you, who privily shall bring in damnable heresies, even denying the Lord that bought them, and bring upon themselves swift destruction.

2 And many shall follow their pernicious ways; by reason of whom the way of truth shall be evil spoken of.

They will speak evil against the truth that these Kingdom Believers have been given! Verse 3:

3 And through covetousness shall they with feigned words make merchandise of you: whose judgment now of a long time lingereth not, and their damnation slumbereth not.

The word "merchandise" is something that is "bought and sold." In other words, there is an exchange of something. How is this possible when Jesus Christ paid the price in full? Think of prosperity preachers. They sell salvation and prosperity for money. They defraud people with false security. Esau gave up his precious birthright for a bowl of porridge because he was hungry. Believers must not treat the Gospel of the Kingdom with such contempt.

Judgment and damnation for these false prophets and preachers is coming!

Peter now lists for the readers a history of God's righteous judgements. He wants to show that He is both willing and able to judge the rebellious. Verses 4-6:

> 4 **For if God spared not the angels that sinned, but cast them down to hell, and delivered them into chains of darkness, to be reserved unto judgment;**
>
> 5 **And spared not the old world, but saved Noah the eighth person, a preacher of righteousness, bringing in the flood upon the world of the ungodly;**
>
> 6 **And turning the cities of Sodom and Gomorrha into ashes condemned them with an overthrow, making them an ensample unto those that after should live ungodly;**

Peter continues with his examples. Remember that "conversation" refers to a "manner of living." Verses 7-8:

7 And delivered just Lot, vexed with the filthy conversation of the wicked: 8 (For that righteous man dwelling among them, in seeing and hearing, vexed his righteous soul from day to day with their unlawful deeds;)

God is more than capable to deliver the godly and to reserve judgment for those who oppose Him. Verses 9-10:

9 The Lord knoweth how to deliver the godly out of temptations, and to reserve the unjust unto the day of judgment to be punished:

10 But chiefly them that walk after the flesh in the lust of uncleanness, and despise government. Presumptuous are they, self-willed, they are not afraid to speak evil of dignities.

Angels are called the great "cloud of witnesses"(Heb. 12:1). The word "railing" means "reproaching or scoffing." Verse 11:

11 Whereas angels, which are greater in power and might, bring not railing accusation against them before the Lord.

Seeing everything, the angels know that the Lord is just, Therefore, they bring no "railing" or accusation against Him.

Peter describes the wickedness of these robbers who seek to deceive and steal their birthright. Verse 12:

> 12 **But these, as natural brute beasts, made to be taken and destroyed, speak evil of the things that they understand not; and shall utterly perish in their own corruption;**

The phrase "natural brute beasts" compares these thieves to animals in the wild. They seek after only their own without regard to others. They have no boundaries to curb their lusts. Verses 13-14:

> 13 **And shall receive the reward of un-righteousness, as they that count it pleasure to riot in the daytime. Spots they are and blemishes, sporting them-selves with their own deceivings while they feast with you;**
>
> 14 **Having eyes full of adultery, and that cannot cease from sin; beguiling unsta-ble souls: an heart they have exercised**

with covetous practices; cursed children:

The children of these deceivers are just like them. Paul wrote to Gentiles who were now saved saying they once lived "in the lusts of our flesh, fulfilling the desires of the flesh and of the mind; and were by nature the children of wrath . . ." (Eph. 2:3). This applies to everyone who rebels against their Creator. Verses 15-16:

15 Which have forsaken the right way, and are gone astray, following the way of Balaam the son of Bosor, who loved the wages of unrighteousness;

16 But was rebuked for his iniquity: the dumb ass speaking with [a] man's voice forbad the madness of the prophet.

Peter makes a broad generalization that applies to all who turn away from or reject God. Verse 17:

17 These are wells without water, clouds that are carried with a tempest; to whom the mist of darkness is reserved for ever.

The book of Revelation ends with a blessing

and a curse concerning the Word of God. These words were written by the Apostle John who we will study next. Revelation 22:18-19:

> 18 **For I testify unto every man that heareth the words of the prophecy of this book, If any man shall add unto these things, God shall add unto him the plagues that are written in this book:**
>
> 19 **And if any man shall take away from the words of the book of this prophecy, God shall take away his part out of the book of life, and out of the holy city, and from the things which are written in this book.**

The words of God's revelation to mankind have been sealed. Nothing can be added and nothing can be taken away. In a world filled with false prophets who teach the multitude a corrupted message, keep this warning in mind. Every teaching should be tested against the unaltered Word of God.

Peter continues about these false teachers and prophets. The word "wantonness" means "seeking after pleasures." They seduce the minds of those formerly saved with enticing words. Verse 18:

18 For when they speak great swelling words of vanity, they allure through <u>the lusts of the flesh</u>, through much <u>wantonness</u>, those that were clean [and had] escaped from them who live in error.

All believers should be cautious for they seek to recapture them – those who were clean and had escaped from the sin of error!

Again, be cautious! They lie. They make empty promises. They serve themselves and they serve the "father of lies." Verse 19:

19 While they promise them liberty, they themselves are the servants of corruption: for of whom a man is overcome, of the same is he brought in [into] bondage.

Our thoughts and our mind is brought under control or, as Peter says, "in bondage" to what we are taught and the messages we accept and believe. Believing God's Word produces one set of results. Rejecting God and His message produce other results contrary to God.

What about the believer who once had faith and now has returned to unbelief? For believing

Jews, it is loss of their salvation. Here is what Peter says about those who do not continue in the faith. Verses 20-21:

> **20 For if after they have escaped the pollutions of the world through the knowledge of the Lord and Saviour Jesus Christ, they are again entangled therein, and overcome, the latter end is worse with them than the beginning.**

> **21 For it had been better for them not to have known the way of righteousness, than, after they have known it, to turn from the holy commandment delivered unto them.**

What about these Jews who were once saved by faith and have become "entangled" again? He says their punishment is worse than if they had never "known the way of righteousness."

He ends by quoting Proverbs 26:11:

> **11 As a dog returneth to his vomit, so a fool returneth to his folly.**

The word "fool" means "one who lacks the ability to reason." The word "mire" means "deep mud" in which someone will get stuck. 2 Peter 2:22:

> 22 But it is happened unto them according to the true proverb, The dog is turned to his own vomit again; and the sow that was washed to her wallowing in the mire.

15

2 Peter 3

Peter stirs up memories of Israel's past. He wants them to remember what was said to them by the prophets of old, the Lord Himself while He was with them, and His apostles. 2 Peter 3:1-2:

> 1 **This second epistle, beloved, I now write unto you; in both which I stir up your pure minds by way of remembrance:**

> 2 **That ye may be mindful of the words which were spoken before by the holy prophets, and of the commandment of us the apostles of the Lord and Saviour:**

With God's revelation to man being completed, Peter warns them about changing what God has said.

He warned them about false teachers and false prophets. The word "scoffer" means "one who contemptuously scorns, mocks, derides, or reproaches." He warns that "in the last days" these "scoffers" will become plentiful. Verses 3-4:

> 3 **Knowing this first, that there shall come in the last days scoffers, walking after their own lusts,**
>
> 4 **And saying, Where is the promise of his coming? for since the fathers fell asleep, all things continue as they were from the beginning of the creation.**

They call into question the promises saying where are these promises now? Nothing has changed.

Psalms 14:1 says, "The fool hath said in his heart, There is no God." Who can make a fool to understand? These scoffers should look. There is evidence that the earth was once flooded and, now, it is no longer flooded. Verses 5-7:

> 5 **For this they willingly are ignorant of, that by the word of God the heavens were of old, and the earth standing out of the water and in the water:**

6 Whereby the world that then was, being overflowed with water, perished:

7 But the heavens and the earth, which are now, by the same word are kept in store, <u>reserved unto fire against the day of judgment and perdition of ungodly men.</u>

The judgment by fire is coming. The Lord has said so and it will happen as He said.

In next verse, I have some personal thoughts I would like to share. As one saved by the Gospel of Grace, I wait in earnest expectation of the blessed hope – the Rapture. If you have read The Glorious Destiny of Israel, you will understand when I ask, "Where are we in the timeline?" Verse 8:

8 But, beloved, be not ignorant of this one thing, that <u>one day is with the Lord as a thousand years, and a thousand years as one day.</u>

Daniel's prophecy recorded in Daniel 9, pinpoints the Crucifixion of the Lord Jesus Christ to 30 A.D. Forty years after His Crucifixion, Jerusalem and the Temple were destroyed by Rome. Why is Peter telling them this? If "one day is with the Lord as a thousand years, and a thousand years as one day," then in 2030 it will be "two days" since 30 A.D. We know that Christ rose from the grave early on the morning of the third day.

We cannot pinpoint the exact date of His Coming. However, we do know that the Rapture occurs seven years prior to His Coming at the same time as the arrival of the Antichrist. Again, this is what I ponder when I sit in front of a fireplace on a cold winter's night. The word "slack" means "remiss or not holding fast." Verse 9:

> 9 The Lord is not slack concerning his promise, as some men count slackness; but is longsuffering to us-ward, not willing that any should perish, but that all should come to repentance.

In the next verse, "the day of the Lord" refers not to one single day, but to a seven-year period called the Tribulation. Verse 10:

> 10 But the day of the Lord will come as a thief in the night; in the which the heavens shall pass away with a great noise, and the elements shall melt with fervent heat, the earth also and the works that are therein shall be burned up.

Compare all this with Matthew 24 where Christ gives a detailed description of the end times. Verses 11-13:

11 Seeing then that all these things shall be dissolved, what manner of persons ought ye to be in all holy conversation and godliness,

12 Looking for and hasting unto the coming of the day of God, wherein the heavens being on fire shall be dissolved, and the elements shall melt with fervent heat?

13 Nevertheless we, according to his promise, look for new heavens and a new earth, wherein dwelleth righteousness.

Do not to confuse "the day of the Lord" with the Apostle Paul's references to "the day of Christ," "the day of Jesus Christ," or "the day of our Lord Jesus Christ." Paul uses these to refer to the day of His Appearing which is the Rapture. However, what Peter just described are the events of the last seven years – the Tribulation.

Peter continues to address true and faithful

Israel who are those saved by the Gospel of the Kingdom. Verse 14:

> 14 **Wherefore, beloved, seeing that ye look for such things, be diligent that ye may be found of [by] him in peace, without spot, and blameless.**

As Peter comes to the end of his second letter, he closes by making a few comments about the Apostle Paul. We know that he was known by the Apostles in Jerusalem. Peter met Paul multiple times and many Jews, both Kingdom Believers and otherwise, were familiar with him. Therefore, he offers no introduction. Verses 15-16:

> 15 **And account that the longsuffering of our Lord is salvation; even as our beloved brother Paul also <u>according to the wisdom given unto him</u> hath written unto you;**

> 16 **As also in all his epistles, speaking in them of these things; in which are some things hard to be understood, which they that are unlearned and unstable wrest, as they do also the other scriptures, unto their own destruction.**

He comments that Paul's doctrine is difficult to understand and for good reason. Paul's Gospel of Grace is different from their Gospel of the Kingdom. However, he warns them that those who "wrest" or "twist" Paul's writings or any other Scripture do so at their own peril.

They should hold fast to the doctrine that they have been given by the prophets, the Christ, and the Twelve Apostles who were eyewitnesses. Verse 17:

> 17 **Ye therefore, beloved, seeing ye know these things before, beware lest ye also, being led away with the error of the wicked, fall from your own stedfastness.**

Finally, as Kingdom Believers, they should grow in the grace given to them. By a strong faith, hold fast to the hope of the promises they have received. They should continue to grow in their knowledge of their Lord and Savior by studying the Word of God. Verse 18:

> 18 **But grow in grace, and in the knowledge of our Lord and Saviour Jesus Christ. To him be glory both now and forever. Amen.**

16

Introduction to John

The Apostle John was one of first disciples chosen by the Lord Jesus Christ along with Peter and James. John was the youngest of the chosen disciples. We know that he was at least thirteen years old. According to Hebrew tradition, the age when a Jewish male is considered to be an adult, marked by a Bar Mitzvah, is age thirteen. He publicly recognizes his responsibility for his actions and his obligation to the Mosaic Law.

We are told that John was the disciple whom Jesus loved. That does not mean that Jesus did not love the others as well, but John had a special place in Jesus' heart. This may have been due to his age. During the Last Supper, John reclined against Jesus. Sitting next to Jesus may indicate John's close connection to Him. This last meal was shared with those who were with Him for three years. They were like family. It was here that Jesus revealed who would betray Him. John 13:20-23

> 20 **Verily, verily, I say unto you, He that receiveth whomsoever I send receiveth me; and he that receiveth me receiveth him that sent me.**
>
> 21 **When Jesus had thus said, he was troubled in spirit, and testified, and said, Verily, verily, I say unto you, that one of you shall betray me.**
>
> 22 **Then the disciples looked one on another, doubting of whom he spake.** 23 **Now there was leaning on Jesus' bosom one of his disciples, whom Jesus loved.**

It was young John who rested upon Him. Peter gets John's attention to ask Jesus a question. Verses 24-26:

> 24 **Simon Peter therefore beckoned to him, that he should ask who it should be of whom he spake.** 25 **He then lying on Jesus' breast saith unto him, Lord, who is it?**

26 Jesus answered, He it is, to whom I shall give a sop, when I have dipped it. And when he had dipped the sop, he gave it to Judas Iscariot, the son of Simon.

Following Jesus' death, He appeared on the shore not far from where the disciples were fishing. After they recognized Him, they came to shore and were greeting by Him. They shared a meal together. It is here where Jesus tells them what they could expect in the future. This provides us with insight about the Apostle John. He records this event for us at the conclusion of his gospel. John 21:15-25:

15 So when they had dined, Jesus saith to Simon Peter, Simon, son of Jonas, lovest thou me more than these? He saith unto him, Yea, Lord; thou knowest that I love thee. He saith unto him, Feed my lambs.

16 He saith to him again the second time, Simon, son of Jonas, lovest thou me? He saith unto him, Yea, Lord; thou knowest that I love thee. He saith unto him, Feed my sheep.

17 He saith unto him the third time,

Simon, son of Jonas, lovest thou me? Peter was grieved because he said unto him the third time, Lovest thou me? And he said unto him, Lord, thou knowest all things; thou knowest that I love thee. Jesus saith unto him, Feed my sheep.

18 Verily, verily, I say unto thee, When thou wast young, thou girdedst thyself, and walkedst whither thou wouldest: but when thou shalt be old, thou shalt stretch forth thy hands, and another shall gird thee, and carry thee whither thou wouldest not. 19 This spake he, signifying by what death he should glorify God. And when he had spoken this, he saith unto him, Follow me.

20 Then Peter, turning about, <u>seeth the disciple whom Jesus loved following; which also leaned on his breast at supper, and said, Lord, which is he that betrayeth thee?</u> 21 <u>Peter seeing him saith to Jesus, Lord, and what shall this man do?</u>

22 Jesus saith unto him, If I will [desire] that he tarry till I come, what is that to thee? follow thou me. 23 Then went this

saying abroad among the brethren, that that disciple should not die: yet Jesus said not unto him, He shall not die; but, If I will that he tarry till I come, what is that to thee?

24 This is the disciple which testifieth of these things, and wrote these things: and we know that his testimony is true.

25 And there are also many other things which Jesus did, the which, if they should be written every one, I suppose that even the world itself could not contain the books that should be written. Amen.

John lived to an old age while he was in exile on the Isle of Patmos. It would be the Apostle John who wrote the final book in the Bible – Revelation. He was chosen by God to see the future. Guided by angels throughout the celestial realm, they showed him things that he found difficult to be put into words. It is this Apostle who we now study in following three epistles. All of these were written to the Jews who are saved by the Kingdom Gospel.

17

1 John 1

John wrote to Kingdom Believers. Many of them were alive during Jesus' earthly ministry. They had seen and heard Him while He was among His people. 1 John 1:1:

> 1 **That which was from the beginning, which we have heard, which we have seen with our eyes, which we have looked upon, and our hands have handled, of the Word of life;**

The word "manifested" means "made known or revealed." Verse 2:

> 2 **(For the life was manifested, and we have seen it, and bear witness, and shew unto you that eternal life, which**

was with the Father, and was manifested unto us;)

For those who had not seen and heard Jesus in person, they could turn to others in their fellowship who had and they could confirm the facts. Verses 3-4:

> 3 <u>That which we have seen and heard declare we unto you,</u> that ye also may have fellowship with us: and truly our fellowship is with the Father, and with his Son Jesus Christ.

> 4 <u>And these things write we unto you, that your joy may be full</u>.

John gives the same message that Jesus gave and it is being confirmed by these witnesses. John uses the word "light" to mean "truth." Verses 5-7:

> 5 This then is the message which we have heard of him, and declare unto you, that <u>God is light</u>, and in him is no darkness at all. 6 If we say that we have fellowship with him, and walk in darkness, we lie, and do not the truth:

> 7 But <u>if we walk in the light, as he is in</u>

the light, [1] **we have fellowship one with another, and [2} the blood of Jesus Christ his Son cleanseth us from all sin.**

John is using an allegory to make his point. Everyone is aware of light and darkness. He writes that "truth" is light and darkness is the absence of light. Therefore, those who reject or deny the light, they are themselves in darkness. Verses 8-10:

> 8 **If we say that we have no sin, we deceive ourselves, and the truth is not in us.** 9 **If we confess our sins, he is faithful and just to forgive us our sins, and to cleanse us from all unrighteousness.** 10 **If we say that we have not sinned, we make him a liar, and his word is not in us.**

Many believers enjoy the simplicity of John's teaching by using allegory. It makes the complex simple and, therefore, is easily grasped and understood.

18

1 John 2

John writes to the beloved children of Abraham who need to be taught the truths of God. 1 John 2:1-2:

1 My little children, these things write I unto you, that ye sin not. And if any man sin, we have an advocate with the Father, Jesus Christ the righteous:

2 And he is the propitiation for our sins: and not for ours only, but also for the sins of the whole world.

The word "propitiation" does not mean payment. Faithful Israel's sins are held in remission. They will be forgiven when their Messiah returns for them. Here, "propitiation" means "the act of appeasing wrath and making peace with an offended person." Payment for their penalty has not yet been applied.

We know that Jesus Christ achieved something no one else could do. His sacrifice was "sufficient" to pay for the sins of all mankind. However, it is only "efficient" or effective if that payment is applied according to God's instructions. For the Jews, the promise is for that payment to be made in the future, however, it is conditional. Those who follow the Gospel of the Kingdom must maintain an living faith as evidenced by their actions. Also, they must "endure unto the end."

John explains this living faith in verses: 3-6:

3 **And hereby we do know that we know him, if we keep his commandments.** 4 **He that saith, I know him, and keepeth not his commandments, is a liar, and the truth is not in him.**

5 **But whoso keepeth his word, in him verily is the love of God perfected: hereby know we that we are in him.** 6 **He that saith he abideth in him ought himself also so to walk, even as he [Christ] walked.**

In other words, the proof of their faith is "in the do-ing." John has not written anything new to them, but reminds them of what they have been told all along. Verse 7:

> 7 Brethren, I write no new commandment unto you, but an old commandment which ye had from the beginning. The old commandment is the word which ye have heard from the beginning.

During the Last Supper, Jesus introduced the New Covenant spoken of by the Prophet Jeremiah. Jeremiah 31:31:

> 31 Behold, the days come, saith the LORD, that <u>I will make a new covenant with the house of Israel, and with the house of Judah</u>:

This is when the New Covenant or New Testament became effective. Matthew 26:26-28:

> 26 And as they were eating, Jesus took bread, and blessed it, and brake it, and gave it to the disciples, and said, Take, eat; this is my body.

27 And he took the cup, and gave thanks, and gave it to them, saying, Drink ye all of it; **28** <u>For this is my blood of the new testament, which is shed for many for the remission of sins.</u>

Jesus Christ did for Israel what they could not do for themselves. He became their Light. He brought light into the darkness and became the Light of the World.

John recorded the words of Jesus introducing a new commandment which sums up the Kingdom Gospel. John 13:34-35:

> **34** <u>A new commandment I give unto you, That ye love one another; as I have loved you, that ye also love one another.</u>
>
> **35** <u>By this shall all men know that ye are my disciples, if ye have love one to another.</u>

When Jesus was questioned by a Pharisee about the greatest commandment, He answers him in Matthew 22:36-40:

> **36** Master, which is the great commandment in the law?

37 Jesus said unto him, Thou shalt love
the Lord thy God with all thy heart, and
with all thy soul, and with all thy mind.
38 This is the first and great commandment.

39 And the second is like unto it, Thou
shalt love thy neighbour as thyself.

40 <u>On these two commandments hang</u>
<u>all the law and the prophets.</u>

In view of the above, it makes sense that John
brings up this "new commandment" since the followers of the Kingdom Gospel must continue to keep
the Law. Christ came not to the change the Law, but
to fulfill it. 1 John 2:8:

8 Again, a new commandment I write
unto you, which thing is true in him and
in you: because <u>the darkness is past,</u>
<u>and the true light now shineth.</u>

The light of the Gospel of the Kingdom which was
promised to Israel has come. They can show their
obedience to Law by loving God and loving their
neighbors. Verses 9-11:

9 He that saith he is in the light, and

hateth his brother, is in darkness even until now.

10 He that loveth his brother abideth in the light, and there is none occasion of stumbling in him.

11 But he that hateth his brother is in darkness, and walketh in darkness, and knoweth not whither [where] he goeth, because that darkness hath blinded his eyes.

John's love for his brethren is evident. He has good news for them. Their sins, according to the promise, will be forgiven. Verses 12-14:

12 I write unto you, little children, because <u>your sins are forgiven you for his name's sake.</u>

13 I write unto you, fathers, because ye have known him that is from the beginning. I write unto you, young men, because ye have overcome the wicked one. I write unto you, little children, because ye have known the Father.

14 I have written unto you, fathers, be-

cause ye have known him that is from the beginning. I have written unto you, young men, because ye are strong, and the word of God abideth in you, and ye have overcome the wicked one.

In 1 Peter 1:16, Peter reminded believers of what God said in Leviticus 11:45:

45 For I am the LORD that bringeth you up out of the land of Egypt, to be your God: ye shall <u>therefore be holy, for I am holy</u>.

Remember, the word "holy" means "separated from the world." It does not mean they must be perfect. We return to our text with 1 John 2:15-17:

15 <u>Love not the world</u>, neither the things that are in the world. If any man love the world, the love of the Father is not in him.

16 <u>For all that is in the world</u>, the lust of the flesh, and the lust of the eyes, and the pride of life, <u>is not of the Father</u>, but is of the world.

17 And <u>the world passeth away</u>, and the

lust thereof: <u>but he that doeth the will of God abideth forever.</u>

John uses the words "the last time" referring to "the end times." The spirit of the antichrists are those who are against God and contrary to the teachings of Christ.

> **18 Little children, it is the last time: and as ye have heard that antichrist shall come, even now are there many antichrists; whereby we know that it is the last time.**

Many of the children of Israel have gone out to be in the world and are not separated from it. Verse 19:

> **19 They went out from us, but they were not of us; for if they had been of us, they would no doubt have continued with us: but they went out, that they might be made manifest [known] that they were not all of us.**

By their actions, they have shown that they have departed from and no longer part of true and faithful Israel.

The word "unction" has a wonderful meaning.

It means "an anointing, a divine or sanctifying gift."
Verse 20:

> 20 But ye have an unction from the Holy
> One, and ye know all things.

This gift is that the truth has been revealed to them.
In other words, they now know the truth! Verse 21:

> 21 I have not written unto you because
> ye know not the truth, but because ye
> know it, and that no lie is of the truth.

The first part of this verse is a double-negative. He is
writing to them because they do know the truth!

John compares those who know the truth with
the others who do not. Verses 22-23:

> 22 Who is a liar but he that denieth that
> Jesus is the Christ? He is antichrist, that
> denieth the Father and the Son.

> 23 Whosoever denieth the Son, the same
> hath not the Father: (but) he that
> acknowledgeth the Son hath the Father
> also.

Scripture tells us that Satan is created being.

God created Lucifer who rebelled against Him. Satan is a liar from the beginning and made himself to be God's enemy. Out of pride, he sought to establishing himself above God. Isaiah 14:12-15:

> 12 **How art thou fallen from heaven, <u>O Lucifer, son of the morning</u>! how art thou cut down to the ground, which didst weaken the nations!**
>
> 13 <u>**For thou hast said in thine heart**</u>**, I will ascend into heaven, I will exalt my throne above the stars of God: I will sit also upon the mount of the congregation, in the sides of the north:**
>
> 14 <u>**I will ascend above the heights of the clouds; I will be like the most High**</u>**.**
>
> 15 **Yet thou shalt be brought down to hell, to the sides of the pit.**

This spirit of rebellion and self-pride are present today on earth. This is the spirit of the antichrist. Both Satan and those who follow him will be eternally punished. You can trust God's Word on that.

John wants the truth that has been revealed to them to remain in them. Truth will never change.

God's Word is the only constant that believers can hold onto. Verses 24-25:

24 **Let that therefore abide in you, which ye have heard from the beginning. If that which ye have heard from the beginning shall remain in you, ye also shall continue in the Son, and in the Father.**

25 **And this is the promise that he hath promised us, even eternal life.**

He cautions them against false prophets and deceivers who want to seduce them. They want them to hold onto their gift of truth. Verses 26-27:

26 **These things have I written unto you concerning them that seduce you.**

27 **But the anointing which ye have received of him [Christ] abideth in you, and ye need not that any man teach you: but as the same anointing teacheth you of all things, and is truth, and is no lie, and even as it hath taught you, ye shall abide in him.**

John wants them to be confident that when Jesus

returns, they will stand before Him unembarrassed. Verse 28:

> 28 **And now, little children, abide in him; that, when he shall appear, we may have confidence, and not be ashamed before him at his coming.**

Knowing that Jesus Christ is righteous, those who are truly born of Him shall be righteous also. Verse 29:

> 29 **If ye know that he is righteous, ye know that every one that doeth righteousness is born of him.**

19

1 John 3

John calls the faithful followers of the Kingdom Gospel by the name "Beloved." They are "sons of God." By hope, they hold onto the truth that has been given to them. This makes them as pure as Christ is pure! 1 John 3:1-3:

> 1 **Behold, what manner of love the Father hath bestowed upon us, <u>that we should be called the sons of God</u>: therefore the world knoweth us not, because it knew him not.**
>
> 2 **Beloved, now are we the sons of God, and it doth not yet appear what we shall be: but we know that, when he shall appear, we shall be like him; for we shall see him as he is.**

3 And every man that hath this hope in him [Christ] purifieth himself, even as he [Christ] is pure.

The word "sin" comes from the Greek word HARMATIA which means "to miss the mark" or "to fall short." Think of an archer striving to hit the bullseye and missing it. That would be a "sin." Now, the Law is the bullseye they must hit. Verses 4-6

4 Whosoever committeth sin transgresseth also the law: for sin is the transgression of the law. 5 And ye know that he was manifested [made known] to take away our sins; and in him is no sin.

6 Whosoever abideth in him sinneth not: whosoever sinneth hath not seen him, neither known him.

How can they recognize a deceiver? John makes it clear in the following verses. Repetition is a useful tool. These epistles are read aloud to the assemblies. Verses 7-9:

7 Little children, let no man deceive you: he that doeth righteousness is righteous, even as he is righteous. [But]

8 He that committeth sin is of the devil; for the devil sinneth from the beginning. For this purpose the Son of God was manifested [made known], that he might destroy the works of the devil.

9 Whosoever is born of God doth not commit sin; for his seed remaineth in him: and he cannot sin, because he is born of God.

He tells them again how to tell the difference between "the children of God" and "the children of the devil." Verses 10-12:

10 In this the children of God are manifest [made known], and the children of the devil: whosoever doeth not righteousness is not of God, neither he that loveth not his brother.

11 For this is the message that ye heard from the beginning, that we should love one another. 12 Not as Cain, who was of that wicked one, and slew his brother. And wherefore slew he him? Because his own works were evil, and his brother's righteous.

When we read the Old Testament, we can see how the people of God were treated by the world. Not only by the Nations, but by the Jews who had lost their faith. This applied to the Christ during His earthly ministry. "He is despised and rejected of men; a man of sorrows, and acquainted with grief" (Isa. 53:3). The brethren should expect nothing different. Verses 13-15:

> 13 **Marvel not, my brethren, if the world hate you. 14 We know that we have passed from death unto life, because we love the brethren. He that loveth not his brother abideth in death.**
>
> 15 **Whosoever hateth his brother is a murderer: and ye know that no murderer hath eternal life abiding in him.**

John teaches that the love of God shown towards them, they should also show towards their brethren. He includes relationships such as husband-wife and parent-child. Verse 16:

> 16 **Hereby perceive we the love of God, because he laid down his life for us: and we ought to lay down our lives for the brethren.**

This certainly applies to the physical needs of fellow-believers.

The word "bowels" refers to "the seat of emotions including kindness, tenderness, and compassion." Those believers with material blessings should share with those believers in need. Verses 17-18:

> 17 **But whoso hath this world's good, and seeth his brother have need, and shutteth up his bowels of compassion from him, how dwelleth the love of God in him?**
>
> 18 **My little children, let us not love in word, neither in tongue; but in deed [doing] and in truth.**

These faithful believers are those who have compassion and show brotherly love. Not just talking about it, but in doing it.

It is by their actions these believers prove they believe. Verses 19-21:

> 19 **And hereby we know that we are of the truth, and shall assure our hearts before him.**

20 For if our heart condemn us, God is greater than our heart, and knoweth all things.

21 Beloved, if our heart condemn us not, then have we confidence toward God.

The "heart" represents the core of a person's being, their thoughts and emotions, who they truly are, and what they truly believe. Therefore, their actions confirm their "heart."

If the believers of the Kingdom Gospel have faith and do the things pleasing to God, then they will be blessed. Nothing has changed since Israel agreed to the Mosaic Covenant. This covenant was conditional. It had consequences often referred to as "the blessings and the curses." These are detailed in the agreement in Deuteronomy 11:26-28:

26 Behold, I set before you this day <u>a blessing and a curse;</u>

27 <u>A blessing, if ye obey the commandments</u> of the LORD your God, which I command you this day:

28 <u>And a curse, if ye will not obey the commandments</u> of the LORD your God

. . .

You can see how this ties in with what John is writing here. 1 John 4:22-24:

> **22 And whatsoever we ask, we receive of him, <u>because we keep his command-ments</u>, and do those things that are pleasing in his sight.**

> **23 And <u>this is his commandment, That we should believe on the name of his Son Jesus Christ, and love one another,</u> as he gave us commandment.**

> **24 And <u>he that keepeth his command ments dwelleth in him, and he in him.</u> And <u>hereby we know that he abideth in us, by the Spirit which he hath given us.</u>**

20

1 John 4

John shows such care and concern for the Kingdom Believers by calling them "little children." His hope is that what they will not be deceived by false teachers. 1 John 4:1:

> 1 Beloved, believe not every spirit, but try the spirits whether they are of God: because many false prophets are gone out into the world.

How are they to know if what they are hearing is true or not? They can test the spirit of the person teaching. Verses 2-3:

> 2 Hereby know ye the Spirit of God: Every spirit that confesseth that Jesus Christ is come in the flesh is of God:

3 And every spirit that confesseth not that Jesus Christ is come in the flesh is not of God: and this is that spirit of antichrist, whereof ye have heard that it should come; and even now already is it in the world.

This method of testing the truth will help shield them from false teachings.

Only believers are of God while others belong to the world. However, they should not be afraid. Verses 4-6:

4 Ye are of God, little children, and have overcome them: because greater is he that is in you, than he that is in the world. **5** They are of the world: therefore speak they of the world, and the world heareth them.

6 We are of God: he that knoweth God heareth us; he that is not of God heareth not us. Hereby know we the spirit of truth, and the spirit of error.

Love is to have an active role in their lives. This has not changed. Jesus shows the importance of love in the lives of Kingdom Believers. Mark 12:29-31:

29 And Jesus answered him, The first of all the commandments is, Hear, O Israel; The Lord our God is one Lord:

30 And <u>thou shalt love the Lord thy God</u> with all thy heart, and with all thy soul, and with all thy mind, and with all thy strength: this is the first commandment.

31 And the second is like, namely this, <u>Thou shalt love thy neighbour as thyself</u>. There is none other commandment greater than these.

John continues with this same theme of love that Jesus taught the Kingdom Believers. 1 John 4:7-8:

7 Beloved, <u>let us love one another:</u> for love is of God; and <u>every one that loveth is born of God</u>, and knoweth God. 8 <u>He that loveth not knoweth not God;</u> for God is love.

John wants them to put love into action. So, he gives the best example they will never forget. Verses 9-10:

9 In this was manifested [made known]

the love of God toward us, because that God sent his only begotten Son into the world, that we might live through him.

10 Herein is love, not that we loved God, but that he loved us, and sent his Son to be the propitiation for our sins.

He wants them to think about this: "If God loved us this much, we too should love each other." Verse 11:

11 Beloved, if God so loved us, we ought also to love one another.

He speaks about God the Father and the special relationship these believers have with Him. Verse 12:

12 No man hath seen God at any time. <u>If we love one another, God dwelleth in us, and his love is perfected in us.</u>

By loving each other, it proves they have the love of Christ dwelling in them. It is that love that perfects them. Verse 13:

13 Hereby know we that we dwell in him, and he in us, because he hath given us of his Spirit.

The Holy Spirit of God dwells in each true believer. It is His presence in them that confirms their active relationship with Him.

They have heard the Kingdom Gospel preached and believed. As proof of this, they obey the commandments of the Lord Jesus Christ. God's love towards them is shown by His actions. In return, they show their love for God by their actions as well. Verses 14-16:

> 14 **And we have seen and do testify that the Father sent the Son to be the Saviour of the world.**
>
> 15 **Whosoever shall confess that Jesus is the Son of God, God dwelleth in him, and he in God.**
>
> 16 **And we have known and believed the love that God hath to us. God is love; and he that dwelleth in love dwelleth in God, and God in him.**

Below, the word "perfect" means "finished, complete; without defective." They can be confident of their salvation in the judgment to come. Verses 17-18:

17 Herein is our love made perfect, that we may have boldness in the day of judgment: because as he is, so are we in this world.

18 There is no fear in love; but perfect love casteth out fear: because fear hath torment. He that feareth is not made perfect in love.

They heard, received, and believed. How is this love perfect? They have no fear and are confident in their relationship with God.

In response, by faith, believers return that love to God by their actions showing that love. Verse 19:

19 <u>We love him, because he first loved us.</u>

How does God know the love is genuine? Real love is authenticated by our actions! They follow His commandment. They are to love God and love the brethren. Verse 20:

20 If a man say, I love God, and hateth his brother, he is a liar: for he that loveth not his brother whom he hath seen, how can he love God whom he

hath not seen?

He closes by reminding them of the first and second commandment concerning fulfilling the Law and the Prophets. Verse 21:

> 21 **And this commandment have we from him, <u>That he who loveth God love his brother also.</u>**

21

1 John 5

Someday, I would like to meet the Apostle John. You can tell a lot about someone from their writing. There are three synoptic gospels and then there is the Gospel of John. He states his purpose in writing it is ". . . that ye might believe that Jesus is the Christ, the Son of God; and that [by] believing ye might have life through his name" (Jn. 20:31).

His reflective temperament gave him an insight into Christ's earthly ministry. He observed everything and this yielded deep thoughts about God and His Son. 1 John 5:1:

> 1 **Whosoever believeth that Jesus is the Christ is born of God: and everyone that loveth him that begat loveth him also that is begotten of him.**

He reminds Kingdom Believers that they show their love for God by loving their brethren and by keeping His commandments. This is proof enough of their faith. Verses 2-3:

> **2 By this we know that we love the children of God, when we love God, and keep his commandments.**
>
> **3 For this is the love of God, that we keep his commandments: and his commandments are not grievous.**

We must not forget that being "holy" means being "separated from the world." Having faith in God gives them victory over the world. Verses 4-5:

> **4 For whatsoever is born of God overcometh the world: and this is the victory that overcometh the world, even [that is to say by] our faith.**
>
> **5 Who is he that overcometh the world, but he that believeth that Jesus is the Son of God?**

Jesus met all the requirements of the Law and was righteous. This included the Jewish ritual of baptism. Matthew 3:13-15:

13 Then cometh Jesus from Galilee to Jordan unto John, to be baptized of him.

14 But John forbad him, saying, I have need to be baptized of thee, and comest thou to me?

15 And Jesus answering said unto him, Suffer [allow] it to be so now: <u>for thus it becometh us to fulfil all righteousness.</u> Then he [John] suffered [allowed] him.

We see the purpose of His baptism in the following. 1 John 5:6-8:

6 This is he that came by water and blood, even Jesus Christ; not by water only, but <u>by water and blood.</u> And it is the Spirit that beareth witness, because the Spirit is truth.

7 For <u>there are three that bear record in heaven, the Father, the Word, and the Holy Ghost: and these three are one.</u>

8 And there are three that bear witness in [on] earth, <u>the Spirit, and the water, and the blood: and these three agree in one.</u>

John's explanation concerning three witnesses in heaven and on earth inspires awe.

The disciples were with Jesus throughout His earthly ministry. They were twelve witnesses, but only men. God is a far greater witness. There is also the innumerable cloud of heavenly witness – the powers, principalities, and rulers of darkness. Everything that was done, was done to meet all the requirements necessary for God to accomplish His plan. A "witness" is "someone who gives testimony to validate the facts in evidence." Verses 9-13:

> 9 **If we receive the witness of men, the witness of God is greater: for this is the witness of God which he hath testified of [concerning] his Son.**
>
> 10 **He that believeth on the Son of God hath the witness in himself: he that believeth not God hath made him a liar; because he believeth not the record that God gave of his Son.**
>
> 11 **And this is the record, that God hath given to us eternal life, and this life is in his Son.** 12 **He that hath the Son hath life; and he that hath not the Son of God hath not life.**

13 These things have I written unto you that believe on the name of the Son of God; that ye may know that ye have eternal life, and that ye may believe on the name of the Son of God.

Their confidence is in the Word of God and by trusting that He is faithful. Believers can ask anything from Him and He hears their petition. Verses 14-15:

14 And this is the confidence that we have in him, that, if we ask anything according to his will, he heareth us:

15 And if we know that he hear us, whatsoever we ask, we know that we have the petitions that we desired of him.

A Sovereign King accepts petitions from His people. He hears them and acts on them according to His will.

In view of their future role as a "nation of priests," John encourages believers to intercede on behalf of other believers. Verses 16-17:

16 If any man see his brother sin a sin which is not unto death, he shall ask,

**and he shall give him life for them that
sin not unto death. There is a sin unto
death: I do not say that he shall pray for
it.**

**17 All unrighteousness is sin: and there
is a sin not unto death.**

John marks the difference between those that "sin
unto death" and those who "sin not unto death." So,
what is the difference?

First of all, this applies to Kingdom Believers
only. The "sin unto death" is the rejection of God. In
other words, the "sin unto death" is what happens to
former believers who have lost their faith. Remember, it is keeping their faith unto the end that saves
them. The "sin not unto death" is any sin committed
by believers who have the faith. John it telling believers that they can pray for that fallen believer. If they
see a believing brother sin, then he should intercede
for them. And, by asking God on their behalf, He
shall give him life because of their request. This
makes sense for two reasons. First, Israel will be a nation of priests in the future interceding for the Nations. Second, look at what James wrote at the close
of his epistle. James 5:16:

16 Confess your faults one to another,

and pray one for another, that ye may be healed. **The effectual fervent prayer of a righteous man availeth much.**

Therefore, righteous brethren are to intercede for their fallen brethren. God will answer the "fervent prayer of a righteous man."

It is God Who will keep the believers with a living faith. It is living because they consistently prove it by their actions. This meets the requirements of the Kingdom Gospel. The world cannot affect the promises God made to them. They are strangers and aliens in a foreign land. Believers are surrounded by the wicked of the world. Yet, they are separated from it because they belong to God. Verses 18-19:

> 18 **We know that whosoever is born of God sinneth not; but he that is begotten of God keepeth himself, and that wicked one toucheth him not.**
>
> 19 **And we know that we are of God, and the whole world lieth in wickedness.**

John reminds the believers of the Gospel of the Kingdom. Jesus Christ is their Messiah and the Son of God. They have been given the gift of knowledge of the truth. As long as they remain connected to the vine, they have life. Jesus said, "I am the vine, ye are the branches: He that abideth in me, and I in him, the same bringeth forth much fruit: for without me ye can do nothing" (Jn. 15:5). If they observe this, then they have confidence and fear not. Verse 20:

20 **And we know that the Son of God is come, and hath given us an understanding, that we may know him that is true, and we are in him that is true, even in his Son Jesus Christ. This is the true God, and eternal life.**

In the last verse, the word "idolize" means "to love or reverence something or someone to the point of adoration." When an object of love or adoration is not God, it is an "idol." John cautions vulnerable believers whom he calls "little children." He warns them to shun anything that would replace their adoration of God and His Son. To do so would jeopardize their salvation. Verses 21:

21 **Little children, keep yourselves from idols. Amen.**

22

2 John 1

As we start 2 John, we need to begin with an explanation. In the salutation, his greeting to those to whom he is writing, he chose the words "unto the elect lady and her children." Some commentators have looked at 3 John in which he addressed that letter to "the well-beloved Gaius." Then, they draw the conclusion that John is writing to an named believer who is a woman. However, I disagree and will leave the decision to you. I believe he is not speaking literally but figuratively. If this is the case, to whom or what does "the elect lady and her children" refer?

Let us look at the text and then we can continue our discussion. John, who is "the elder," begins his letter with 2 John 1:1:

1 The elder unto <u>the elect lady and her children</u>, whom I love in the truth; and not I only, but also all they that have known the truth;

I believe the "lady" is the bride of Christ and "her children" are those who are true and faithful Israel – those who now know "the truth." Bear with me. John used the words "the elect lady and her children." The word "elect," when used in connection with Israel, means "the Chosen." Israel was chosen out of the other nations. In the Wilderness, God, through Moses, set Israel apart as a peculiar people. Deuteronomy 14:1-2:

> **1** Ye are <u>the children of the LORD your God</u> . . . **2** For <u>thou art an holy people unto the LORD thy God</u>, and <u>the LORD hath chosen thee to be a peculiar people unto himself</u>, above all the nations that are upon the earth.

Look at their position relative to the other nations! God has "chosen thee to be a peculiar people unto himself, above all the nations." He elected them.

This "peculiar" people have a purpose. Remember, the word "peculiar" means "belonging to a person and only that person." God has plans for them in His Kingdom. Exodus 19:3-6:

> **3 And Moses went up unto God, and the LORD called unto him out of the mountain, saying, Thus shalt thou say to the house of Jacob, and tell the children of Israel;**

> **4 Ye have seen what I did unto the Egyptians, and how I bare you on eagles' wings, and brought you unto myself.**

> **5 Now therefore, if ye will obey my voice indeed, and keep my covenant, then ye shall be a peculiar treasure unto me above all people: for all the earth is mine:**

> **6 <u>And ye shall be unto me a kingdom of priests, and an holy nation</u>. These are the words which thou shalt speak unto <u>the children of Israel</u>.**

God referred to them as "the children of Israel." I believe we can be confident that "her children" are the true believers of Israel – the ones saved by the truth. John called them "her" children. They belong to this elect "lady." We will return to this shortly.

John continues his letter by blessing "the elect lady and her children" who have the truth, now revealed, dwells in them. 2 John 1:2-3:

> 2 **For the truth's sake, which dwelleth in us, and shall be with us forever.**
>
> 3 **Grace be with you, mercy, and peace, from God the Father, and from the Lord Jesus Christ, the Son of the Father, in truth and love.**

Do you recall what John wrote earlier? In a previous letter, he used the word "unction." The word "unction" means "an anointing, a divine or sanctifying gift." 1 John 2:20:

> 20 **But ye have an unction from the Holy One, and ye know all things.**

We were told this gift is the gift of truth. In other words, they now know the truth! Verse 21:

> 21 **I have not written unto you because ye know not the truth, but because ye know it, and that no lie is of the truth.**

He is writing to them because they do know the truth!

Now, we are ready to resume our text where John continues his theme on "truth." Notice, again, the "lady and her children." 2 John 1:4-5:

> 4 I rejoiced greatly that I found of thy children walking in truth, <u>as we have received a commandment from the Father.</u>

> 5 And now I beseech thee, lady, not as though I wrote a new commandment unto thee, but <u>that which we had from the beginning, that we love one another.</u>

This is not something new. They have been told this from the beginning. Christ taught this in His earthly message and the Hebrews epistles reinforce it. Verse 6:

> 6 And this is love, that we walk after his commandments. This is the commandment, That, as ye have heard from the beginning, ye should walk in it.

There will be numerous frauds and swindlers who will try to deceive them and take away the truth they received. Verse 7-8:

7 For many deceivers are entered into the world, who confess not that Jesus Christ is come in the flesh. This is a deceiver and an antichrist.

8 Look to [after] yourselves, that we lose not those things which we have wrought [accomplished], but that we receive a full reward.

They need to safeguard what they have already accomplished. Failing to do so will cause them to lose their salvation.

How can one determine if what someone is saying is true? They must test this person. We have heard the saying that "actions speak louder than words." So, it is not what they are saying, but what they are doing that will show who they are. Second, those who are telling the truth will not refute sound doctrine. This is the same argument that John has been making on behalf of Christ. Verses 9-11:

9 Whosoever transgresseth, and abideth not <u>in the doctrine of</u> Christ, hath not God. He that abideth <u>in the doctrine of Christ</u>, he hath both the Father and the Son.

10 If there come any unto you, and bring not this doctrine, receive him not into your house, neither bid him God speed:

11 For he that biddeth him God speed is partaker of his evil deeds.

John has finished with what he wants to say. He intends on coming to visit them face to face and sharing in fellowship. Verse 12:

12 Having many things to write unto you, I would not write with paper and ink: but I trust to come unto you, and speak face to face, that our joy may be full.

It is common practice when writing from one assembly to another to include greetings from one group of believers to the other. I believe the final verse ties in with the first which referred to "the elect lady and her children." Verse 13:

13 The children of thy elect sister greet thee. Amen.

These sisters share a commonality that unites them. These believers are like two sisters. John includes himself in the group of believers who have received the truth. These two fellowships of believers share a common truth, promise, and destiny. All Scripture is true. Sometimes the interpretation of minor details are open for discussion among the believers.

Personal Comments:

These notes are for readers interested in my personal thoughts on "the elect lady and her children" (2 Jn. 1:1).

I believe the "elect lady and her children" figuratively represent true and faithful Israel. God created Israel to become a holy nation, a "peculiar" people, chosen or elected by God for His own purpose. God chose them. They are His Elect.[5]

When God completes the restoration of His Creation, and He will, Israel will perform a vital function. As a "nation of priests," they will intercede on behalf of the "other nations." They will serve in God's earthly temple in Jerusalem on God's behalf. The Apostle John wrote the Gospel of John, three epistles, and the book of Revelation. In the latter, he

---

[5] I go into greater detail about Israel's future in *The Glorious Destiny of Israel: The Fulfillment of God's Promises and Prophecies to Israel.*

tells us about the bride and bridegroom. Revelation 19:6-8:

6 And I heard as it were the voice of a great multitude, and as the voice of many waters, and as the voice of mighty thunderings, saying, Alleluia: for the Lord God omnipotent reigneth.

7 Let us be glad and rejoice, and give honour to him: <u>for the marriage of the Lamb is come,</u> <u>and his wife hath made herself ready</u>.

8 And to her [His wife] was granted that she should be arrayed in fine linen, clean and white: for the fine linen is the righteousness of saints.

John the Baptist identified Jesus Christ as "the Lamb of God." In the following, the Apostle John writes about "the Lamb" and "His wife." Verse 9:

9 And he saith unto me, Write, Blessed are they which are called unto <u>the marriage supper of the Lamb</u> . . .

This discussion changes nothing concerning Israel salvation or their future. Some believe that the

Church (the Body of Christ) is the bride of Christ. I do not. The Body of Christ is comprised of those who are saved by the Gospel of Grace. They were removed by Jesus Christ at the Rapture.[6] The Body of Christ is "His Body" and not His wife.

Personally, and I say this in jest, I think a nice Jewish boy deserves to have a nice Jewish girl for his wife. However, I still think this needs to be interpreted figuratively and not literally. Consider further what John records in Revelation 21:1-3:

> 1 **And I saw a new heaven and a new earth: for the first heaven and the first earth were passed away; and there was no more sea.**
>
> 2 **And <u>I John saw the holy city, new Jerusalem, coming down from God out of heaven, prepared as a bride adorned for her husband.</u>**
>
> 3 **And I heard a great voice out of heaven saying, Behold, <u>the tabernacle of God is with men, and he will dwell with them, and they shall be his people, and God</u>**

---

[6] I go into great detail about the Gospel of Grace in *Letters To Theophilus: Are You Ready For The End Times?*

himself shall be with them, and be their God.

I believe the bride of Christ is the New Jerusalem. She is the "elect lady. True and faithful Israel is "her children." Her children will dwell within her which is the New Jerusalem. Her husband will be the King Who reigns over them forever.

Again, this is just speculation. I will end with a quote from the Prophet Isaiah. He delivered this prophecy to God's "elect children." Isaiah 64:4:

> 4 **For since the beginning of the world men have not heard, nor perceived by the ear, neither hath the eye seen, O God, beside thee, what he hath prepared for him that waiteth for him.**

23

3 John 1

John calls himself "the elder" as he writes to Gaius, a friend and fellow believer in the truth. It appears that he was introduced to the truth by John. Having received news from others that he continues in the faith brings him joy. 3 John 1:1-4:

1 [John] The elder unto the wellbeloved Gaius, whom I love in the truth.

2 Beloved, I wish above all things that thou mayest prosper and be in health, even as thy soul prospereth.

3 For I rejoiced greatly, when the brethren came and testified of the truth that is in thee, even as thou walkest in the

truth. 4 I have no greater joy than to hear that my children walk in truth.

He compliments Gaius because his manner of living is proof of his active faith. His charity or godly love is spoken about within the fellowship. By living like this, he encourages others to do the same in their own lives. Verses 5-6:

5 Beloved, thou doest faithfully whatsoever thou doest to the brethren, and to strangers; 6 Which [Who] have borne witness [spoken] of thy charity before the church: whom if thou bring forward on their journey after a godly sort, thou shalt do well:

Gaius was doing good "to the brethren and to strangers" implies that he was charitable towards both the believers and to others. He takes nothing from them in the way of a payment. All he does is done as an act of love without asking for anything in return. His love for God is shown by loving his neighbors. Verse 7:

7 Because that for his name's sake they went forth, taking nothing of the Gentiles. 8 We therefore ought to receive such, that we might be fellow-helpers

to the truth.

He tells Gaius how he contacted a local fellowship near him with a leader named Diotrephes. He describes this man and his actions. Verses 9-10:

> 9 I wrote unto the church: but Diotrephes, who loveth to have the preeminence among them, receiveth us not.

> 10 Wherefore, if I come, I will remember his deeds which he doeth, prating against us with malicious words: and not content therewith, neither doth he himself receive the brethren, and forbiddeth them that would, and casteth them out of the church.

The word "prating" means "to talk a lot about nothing important, to run on and on." He appears to have made it his own church. This assembly would not benefit Gaius whose own work deserves honorable mention.

Who he follows should be determined by their actions whether they be good or evil. Verse 11:

> 11 Beloved, follow not that which is evil,

but that which is good. He that doeth good is of God: but he that doeth evil hath not seen God.

John hears good things about Demetrius from others and he can trust him. Verse 12:

12 Demetrius hath good report of [from] all men, and of the truth itself: yea, and we also bear record; and ye know that our record is true.

John closes his letter by stating that he will tell Gaius more when he sees him face to face. He blesses him and exchanges greetings between fellow Kingdom Believers. Verse 13:

13 I had many things to write, but I will not with ink and pen write unto thee:

14 But I trust I shall shortly see thee, and we shall speak face to face. Peace be to thee. Our friends salute thee. Greet the friends by name.

24

Introduction to Jude

Not much is known about Jude other than he is the author of the epistle by the same name. There have been debates over his identity. The name "Jude" is a derivation of the name "Judas." Here, we must not confuse him with Judas Iscariot, who betrayed Jesus Christ. Jude is an honorable name. It goes back to the beginning of Israel. "Abraham begat Isaac; and Isaac begat Jacob; and Jacob begat Judas and his brethren" (Matt. 1:2).

He does begin his letter by stating apostolic authority. He simply says that he is the "brother of James" (Jude 1:1). There is evidence that he was called to be an apostle in Luke 6:13-16:

13 And when it was day, he called unto

him his disciples: and of them <u>he chose</u> <u>twelve, whom also he named apostles;</u>

14 Simon, (whom he also named Peter,) and Andrew his brother, James and John, Philip and Bartholomew, 15 Matthew and Thomas, James the son of Alphaeus, and Simon called Zelotes, 16 <u>And Judas the brother of James</u>, and Judas Iscariot, which also was the traitor.

Jude is also called "Juda." He was both the bother of the Apostle James and the half-brother of Jesus Christ. We gain this information from a question asked by men who were local to the area where Jesus grew up. Therefore, these men were familiar with His parents and family. Mark 6:1-3:

1 And he went out from thence, and came into his own country; and his disciples follow him.

2 And when the sabbath day was come, he began to teach in the synagogue: and many hearing him were astonished, saying, From whence hath this man these things? and what wisdom is this which is given unto him, that even such mighty works are wrought by his

hands?

3 Is not this the carpenter, the son of Mary, <u>the brother of James, and Joses, and of Juda</u>, and Simon? and are not his sisters here with us? And they were offended at him.

Jude is writing to Jews saved by the Gospel of the Kingdom referring to their "common salvation." Those who are true and faithful Israel have received the truth. They share in the same promise of salvation – the same hope of the coming Kingdom.

He reminds his readers of the truths they hold and warns them about deceivers who spread falsehoods among the brethren. As such, he encourages them to defend their faith and remain committed to the truth. They must keep the faith and continue to prove their faith through their actions. Finally, they must remember what their Messiah said, "But he that shall endure unto the end, the same shall be saved" (Matt. 24:13).

25

Jude 1

Jude is writing to those who God has separated from the world by the Gospel of the Kingdom. The word "called" has a particular meaning that is often misunderstood. It means "invited or summoned." However, if someone is invited or summoned, it does not necessarily mean they will accept that invitation or appear as requested. We all have free will to choose. All of Israel is invited, but not all will accept the invitation. Jude 1:1-2:

> 1 **Jude, the servant of Jesus Christ, and brother of James, to them that are sanctified by God the Father, and preserved in Jesus Christ, and called: 2 Mercy unto you, and peace, and love, be multiplied.**

Jude is writing to those who have accepted

the Gospel of the Kingdom by faith. They confessed that Jesus Christ is their Messiah and the Son of God. They have repented and turned from their sins. Baptized as a public confession of their faith, they remain committed to following the Law of Moses. These are the Kingdom Believers and they share in the same salvation. Verse 3:

> 3 **Beloved, when I gave all diligence to write unto you of <u>the common salvation</u>, it was needful for me to write unto you, and exhort you that ye should earnestly contend for <u>the faith</u> which was once delivered unto the saints.**

There are some within their fellowship who have joined them, but are contrary to the truth. Not all Jews will accept the invitation from God. Some will only appear to accept the truth. Verse 4:

> 4 **For there are certain men crept in unawares, who were before of old ordained to this condemnation, ungodly men, turning the grace of our God into lasciviousness, and denying the only Lord God, and our Lord Jesus Christ.**

Jude reminds them not to forget what they know. Israel has a history with God that they must not forget. He gives three examples of those who rejected or did not believe God. They were judged and received just punishment. Verses 5-7:

> **5 I will therefore put you in remembrance, though ye once knew this, how that the Lord, having saved the people out of the land of Egypt, afterward <u>destroyed them that believed not</u>.**

> **6 And the angels which kept not their first estate, but left their own habitation, he hath <u>reserved in everlasting chains under darkness unto the judgment</u> of the great day.**

> **7 Even as Sodom and Gomorrha, and the cities about them in like manner, giving themselves over to fornication, and going after strange flesh, are <u>set forth for an example, suffering the vengeance of eternal fire</u>.**

God is merciful and patient, but He has limits. Once those limits are crossed, He is justified to punish the rebellious and disobedient.

He continues with additional poignant examples. Verses 8-9:

8 Likewise also these filthy dreamers defile the flesh, despise dominion, and speak evil of dignities.

9 Yet Michael the archangel, when contending with the devil he disputed about the body of Moses, durst not bring against him a railing accusation, but said, <u>The Lord rebuke thee.</u>

When Moses died, Michael, the archangel, was sent by God to retrieve his body. Satan wanted his body and there was an argument over it. Michael, acknowledging Satan's former station, left his rebuke to God. Moses will play an important role in Israel's future. I am one of many who believe Moses will be one of the two witnesses in Revelation. God will use these two witnesses during the early Tribulation to warn others of the coming judgment.

These false believers who are among the fellowships contend against the faithful. They are no different than Satan, the father of lies. The word "brute" means "without sense, irrational, animalistic in nature." Verse 10:

10 But these speak evil of those things which they know not: but what they know naturally, as brute beasts, in

those things they corrupt themselves.

The word "gainsaying" means "to contradict or oppose in words; to deny or declare not to be true." Verse 11:

> 11 **Woe unto them! for they have gone in the way of Cain, and ran greedily after the error of Balaam for reward, and perished in the gainsaying of Core.**

Gainsayers are those who challenge God and the Word of God. Jude cites Core, also Korah, as an example. He led a rebellion against Moses and Aaron both of whom God had appointed. Although some were not from the tribe of Levi and not eligible, they wanted to claim by force, contrary to God's expressed instructions, the authority of the priesthood. Needless to say, it did not work out for them. (See Num. 16:1-40.)

These gainsayers are in the fellowship with the sincere believers. This includes their holidays and feasts. Verse 12:

> 12 **These are spots in your feasts of charity, when they feast with you, feeding themselves without fear [respect]: [Like] clouds they are without water,**

carried about of winds; trees whose fruit withereth, without fruit, twice dead, plucked up by the roots;

Jude uses the words "twice dead." They are spiritually dead because they reject life. Then, they will die a physical death. They choose to reject God and His truth during in this life. He will reject them after their physical death – a spiritual separation from God for eternity.

Picture billowing waves driven by the winds to-and-fro and stars who have left their posts. Spiritual eternity without God is like "the blackness of darkness forever." Verse 13:

13 Raging waves of the sea, foaming out their own shame; wandering stars, to whom is reserved the blackness of darkness forever.

Scoffers will continue asking, "Where is this day of the Lord? Where is this judgment?" They have chosen to reject God's warnings going back as far as Enoch. The Word of God never changes. Verses 14-15:

14 And Enoch also, the seventh from Adam, prophesied of these, saying, Be-

hold, the Lord cometh with ten thousands of his saints,

15 To execute judgment upon all, and to convince all that are ungodly among them of all their ungodly deeds which they have ungodly committed, and of all their hard speeches which ungodly sinners have spoken against him.

Jude hopes that his description of these gainsayers will move true and faithful Israel to action. They must protect themselves against those who do not follow the truth of God. Verses 16-19:

16 These are murmurers, complainers, walking after their own lusts; and their mouth speaketh great swelling words, having men's persons in admiration because of advantage.

17 But, beloved, remember ye the words which were spoken before of the apostles of our Lord Jesus Christ;

18 How that they told you there should be mockers in the last time, who should walk after their own ungodly lusts.

19 **These be they who separate them-selves, sensual, having not the Spirit.**

These are cancerous sores within their own company. John urges them to protect themselves against them. They should focus on building their knowledge of God and teaching others. Verse 20:

20 **But ye, beloved, building up your-selves on your most holy faith, praying in the Holy Ghost,**

21 **Keep yourselves in the love of God, looking for the mercy of our Lord Jesus Christ unto eternal life.**

Some of those faithful souls who contended against God and His doctrine could possibly be redeemed and returned to fellowship. Verses 22-23:

22 **And of some have compassion, mak-ing a difference:**

23 **And others save with fear, pulling them out of the fire; hating even the gar-ment spotted by the flesh.**

Jude closes with this wonderful blessing upon believers who wait with hope for the Kingdom. They hold onto the promises of God by trusting in His Word. They continue to demonstrate their faith by the proof of their actions. Verses 24-25:

24 Now unto him that is able to keep you from falling, and to present you faultless before the presence of his glory with exceeding joy,

25 To the only wise God our Saviour, be glory and majesty, dominion and power, both now and ever. Amen.

Epilogue

At the end of a book, I would like to share some personal comments about what I learned while writing this book. No matter how much we think we know, we will never know everything. This applies especially to the Word of God. Generally, we cannot help by gain a deeper understanding of the text when we view it within the context of Scripture. What do I mean by this?

How many people do you know have started the year with a resolution to read the whole Bible? However, when we see Scripture through the lens of right-division, we suddenly see it in the way God intended Scripture to be seen. The Age of Grace was a mystery. God had hidden it from everyone until it was revealed to Paul by the Risen Lord. Therefore, it must stand apart from the Scripture that applies to the Jews – the children of Abraham. Similarly, when we study Scripture outside the Pauline epistles, they too must stands apart. This includes the Law, the Prophets, and the Writings. To this, we can add the

Four Gospels, Hebrews, the seven Hebrew epistles, and Revelation. These books can be grouped together. I am sure that this simplification will upset many people. However, I am trying to present a broad view of Scripture to assist both Jews and non-Jews. Everyone is welcome to make their own generalizations. I have found the deep riches of God's Word by writing dividing the Word of Truth. (See 2 Tim. 2:15.)

I would like to make comments directed to each of two groups. The first is to those who follow the Gospel of Grace. They are saved by grace which is a gift of God. They receive His gracious gift by believing His offer. Their salvation is immediate upon believing and their faith activates their salvation. There is no requirement for works. Grace Believers be careful. Do not mix the Gospel of Grace with the Gospel of the Kingdom. The latter is not being offered to you. It belongs solely to the children of Abraham.

The Grace Gospel is simple and it stands separate from the Kingdom Gospel. Anything added to the Gospel of Grace goes beyond altering it. It does not make it another gospel . . .it voids it! This is what the believers in Galatia were doing when Paul wrote them. Galatians 1:6-7

6 I marvel that ye are so soon removed from him that called you into the grace of Christ <u>unto another gospel</u>: **7** <u>Which is not another</u>; but there be some that trouble you, and would pervert the gospel of Christ.

Notice his stern warning to those who alter the Gospel of Grace. It is a very powerful warning; so important that Paul says it twice. Verses 8-9:

8 But though we, or an angel from heaven, preach <u>any other gospel</u> unto you than that which we have preached unto you, <u>let him be accursed</u>.

9 As we said before, so say I now again, <u>If any man preach any other gospel unto you than that ye have received, let him be accursed</u>.

Through the Apostle Paul, God made the Gospel of Grace available to the Jews first and then to the Greeks or Gentiles. So, it is available to everyone. Those interested in a detailed explanation, consider reading *Letters To Theophilus* listed in the back of this book. The Gospel of Grace is presently available to everyone; not so with the Kingdom Gospel! That offer was extended to the lost sheep of the house of

Israel alone. (See Matt. 10:2-7.)

The Gospel of the Kingdom is only available to the lost sheep of the House of Israel. Let us confirm this to be true. To whom was the New Covenant promised? We see that it is very specific in Jeremiah 31:31-32:

> 31 **Behold, the days come, saith the LORD, that <u>I will make a new covenant with the house of Israel, and with the house of Judah</u>:**
>
> 32 **Not according to <u>the covenant that I made with their fathers</u> in the day that I took them by the hand <u>to bring them out of the land of Egypt</u>; which my covenant they brake, although I was an husband unto them, saith the LORD:**

The offer of the New Covenant was officially announced at the Last Supper. Jesus Christ came "to confirm the promises made unto the fathers" (Rom. 15:8). Notice the use of the word "fathers" in verse 32 above.

Consider all the commandments that Jesus taught His disciples while on earth. These Kingdom Apostles are to carry this message, this Gospel of the

Kingdom, to the children of Israel. This was to fulfill the promises made to the fathers. (See Rom. 15:8.) Notice His instructions given to the Eleven at His Ascension. Matthew 28:19-20:

> 19 **Go ye therefore, and teach all nations, baptizing them in the name of the Father, and of the Son, and of the Holy Ghost:**
>
> 20 <u>**Teaching them to observe all things whatsoever I have commanded you:**</u> **and, lo, I am with you alway, even unto the end of the world. Amen.**

Later the Ascension, the Kingdom Apostles see Jesus face to face before His departure. The establishment of the kingdom is still forefront in their minds. Look at the question they asked Him. Acts 1:6:

> 6 **When they therefore were come together, <u>they asked of him, saying, Lord, wilt thou at this time restore again the kingdom to Israel?</u>**

He did not give them an answer, because the kingdom would be delayed because of Israel's unbelief. Verse 7:

7 And he said unto them, It is not for you to know the times or the seasons, which the Father hath put in his own power.

Israel consistently showed lack of faith. Read Peter's speech on Pentecost in Acts 2. Here is some of those verses. Acts 2:36-38:

36 <u>Therefore let all the house of Israel know assuredly, that God hath made that same Jesus, whom ye have crucified, both Lord and Christ.</u>

37 Now when they heard this, they were pricked in their heart, and said unto Peter and to the rest of the apostles, Men and brethren, what shall we do?

38 Then Peter said unto them<u>, Repent, and be baptized every one of you in the name of Jesus Christ for the remission of sins, and ye shall receive the gift of the Holy Ghost.</u>

The message preached to the Jews by the Apostle Peter and the others remained unchanged. Without understanding this, their message becomes obfuscated.

Friend, I hope this study brought you a deeper

understanding of the seven Hebrew epistles. I love studying the Word of Truth and sharing it with others. May God fill you with the understanding of His Word.

God bless you,
Dr. David Alan Greene

Other GraceWord Publications

Cartas A Teofilo
Efesios: Dispensacionalmente considerado
El evangelio Oculto: Una vez fue un misterio . . .

About the Author

Dr. David Alan Greene has over thirty-five years of experience as an insurance agent selling both property and casualty as well as life insurance. During his career, he taught and explained the content and meaning of policies to his clients. Now retired, he devotes much of his time to teaching the Bible.

He obtained his Bachelor of Theology, Master of Biblical Studies, and Ph.D. in Biblical Studies from Evangelical Theological Seminary where he holds the position of Dean of Graduate Studies. He also holds a Ph.D. in Christian Counseling. He has written numerous biblical commentaries and books on rightly dividing the Word of Truth.

www.ingramcontent.com/pod-product-compliance
Lightning Source LLC
Chambersburg PA
CBHW060801120626
46557CB00001B/55